The Art of Fasting

Becoming a more prayerful person

Matthew Porter

Copyright © 2025 Matthew Porter

First published 2025 by Authentic Media Limited,
PO Box 6326, Bletchley, Milton Keynes, MK1 9GG.
authenticmedia.co.uk

The right of Matthew Porter to be identified as the Author of this Work
has been asserted in accordance with the
Copyright, Designs and Patents Act 1988.

All rights reserved.
No part of this publication may be reproduced, stored
in a retrieval system, or transmitted in any form or by any means,
electronic, mechanical, photocopying, recording or otherwise, without
the prior permission of the publisher or a licence permitting restricted
copying. In the UK such licences are issued by the Copyright Licensing
Agency, 5th Floor, Shackleton House, 4 Battle Bridge Lane, London SE1 2HX.

British Library Cataloguing in Publication Data
A catalogue record for this book is available from the British Library.
ISBN: 978-1-78893-369-8
978-1-78893-370-4 (e-book)

Scripture quotations taken from
The Holy Bible, New International Version Anglicised
Copyright © 1979, 1984, 2011 Biblica
Used by permission of Hodder & Stoughton Ltd, an Hachette UK company.
All rights reserved.
'NIV' is a registered trademark of Biblica
UK trademark number 1448790.

Cover design by Henry Milne

Fasting is something I know I ought to do more and I feel guilty that I don't. Having read this book, I find myself wanting to fast and, for the first time ever, excited by the prospect. Matthew so helpfully unpacks the art of fasting, not only explaining why fasting should be a regular part of our spiritual diet but also giving practical and realistic help to actually do it.

James Grier, Bishop of Plymouth, Diocese of Exeter, UK

I am so grateful that Matthew Porter has written *The Art of Fasting* to invite you to discover this beautiful pathway into greater intimacy with Jesus. Fasting is a lost art that needs to be recovered in the church today and Matthew helps do just that. He brings unique perspectives to the table that include practical insights to help equip you on your fasting journey no matter where your starting point is. As you dive in and embrace a lifestyle of fasting and prayer, may you be inspired, transformed and ignited with fresh hunger for God.

Jennifer Miskov PhD, author of Fasting for Fire and founding Director of School of Revival, USA

I am delighted to commend this book to you having enjoyed it and been enriched by it in my own thinking about and practice of fasting and its place in Christian discipleship. Bishop Matthew writes in a characteristically warm, authentic and engaging way, drawing on his own lived experience and also the wisdom of the ages from across a wonderful diversity of Christian traditions. Matthew brings together rich theological reflection and good practical guidance that will indeed help the reader to become a more fruitful and fulfilled missional disciple of Jesus. This is a rich resource that will repay being returned to often.

Mark Davies, Bishop of Middleton,
Greater Manchester, UK

Have we lost the centrality of fasting as part of our walk with Christ? I know I certainly had! This wonderful book, a collection of wisdom from across the ages, has inspired and moved me. It has taken me from being a non-faster to a faster, and I am so grateful. And if you want a closer connection with God and revival, I encourage you to take a few hours to read this.

Emma Buchan, Head of the Churches and Networks Support Team, Church of England, UK

In this provocative and thoughtful exploration of fasting, Matthew Porter champions this often-neglected discipline as an essential element of the prayer life of every disciple of Jesus. Through Scripture and the wisdom of Christian writers down the ages, alongside the personal reflections of ordinary followers of Jesus gathered from his years of ministry, Matthew challenges us all to make fasting part of our toolkit for living for Christ, and turns abstinence into real food for thought.

Simon Cook, Area Dean of Bolton,
Greater Manchester, UK

Contents

Preface	vii
Introduction	1
1. Mouth	12
2. Heart	42
3. Hands	70
4. Knees	102
5. Feet	122
Afterword	147
Acknowledgements	149
Resources	150
Notes	152
Index of People	167

Preface

This book is written to help followers of Jesus become more prayerful through the practice of fasting.

It is called *The Art of Fasting* because discipleship – the daily practice of following Jesus – is more an art than a science. It's not a technical process, based on logic or analytical deduction. It's not about rigidly adhering to laws or rules about behaviour or piety. It's more like learning a musical instrument, or discovering how to paint, both of which require patient practice. You have to give yourself to it: particularly your energy and emotions, as well as your time and talents. This is the stretching and adventurous life of discipleship into which followers of Jesus are invited, empowered by the Holy Spirit. It's thoroughly relational – loving God and loving people – and beautifully creative, cultivating habits of the heart which result in a lifestyle that brings lasting transformation to us and to the world. Eugene H. Peterson, author of *The Message* version of the Bible, summarised such a life as 'learning the unforced rhythms of grace'.[1]

This book, in *The Art of* series, is about a particular rhythmic feature of discipleship – *The Art of Fasting*. In a few pages the habit is explained and explored, with readers encouraged to practise this art in order to mature and impact the world. I think you will enjoy it. But most of all, I hope this habit helps you become a more fruitful and fulfilled missional disciple of Jesus.

The Art of Fasting is the third in a series of books about discipleship habits.

Matthew Porter
Bishop of Bolton

Introduction

This is a book about learning prayerfulness through fasting. It's about becoming more reliant on God by *not* eating.

Lots of people are talking about fasting these days. For example, I was recently radio-channel surfing while driving and I stumbled across an intriguing interview on Radio 4's *Woman's Hour* with Saira Hameed from Imperial College, London. For health reasons Dr Hameed was advocating careful, considered, regular times when we don't eat, saying that fasting can help our physical, mental and emotional health, enabling us to think, work, sleep, live and love better. It was fascinating. Also, people are writing about fasting. While millions of cookbooks are sold each year telling us how to enjoy eating, there's a growing trend for books on how to enjoy *not* eating,[1] and this book adds to the collection.

Food

The Radio 4 show, coupled with the books on eating and not eating, got me thinking more broadly about our relationship with food, realising how foundational cooking and eating have always been in the lives of human beings.

Food is so central to each of our *individual* lives. We need it to survive, with the average Western person devoting four years of their life to eating,[2] yet if we consume too much food, or the wrong kind, we can easily damage ourselves. Some therefore restrict their diet, choosing perhaps to be vegetarian, vegan, or pescatarian. I have friends who do this, mainly for health reasons, although for others it's an ethical or religious choice. Also, a growing number find food very troublesome, as they struggle with eating disorders which negatively affect not only their bodies, but their minds and emotions too.

Food is also central to our *communal* lives. Think about it, when we gather with loved ones, so often it's around a dining table. Many of the pleasures associated with eating come not only from its consumption but its preparation, which are often shared with others, fostering learning and social bonding. Even though we now spend only half the time in food preparation than we used to,[3] this social side to cooking is still significant, building friendship and community cohesion.

So, given this basic importance of food, why fast?

Prayer
Among the many positive reasons for fasting, one that's often missed in contemporary literature or radio programmes is that it's *best practised as a discipline of prayer*. For thousands of years and still today, the majority

Introduction

of people have linked fasting with praying. This book entitled *The Art of Fasting* aims to help readers see this, recognising that for all the helpful benefits of fasting – of which there are many – the *best* thing is that it helps our prayers. That's why this book is subtitled: *Becoming a more prayerful person*.

If you want to become more prayerful, then it stands to reason that you should start praying, but there's an additional habit that energises prayer like no other: the discipline of fasting. So start fasting. In the same way that regular giving is the foundational discipline which helps us become more generous (see my book *The Art of Giving*), and journalling is the key discipline which helps us become more reflective (see my book *The Art of Journalling*), so this book will show that fasting is the strategic discipline which helps us become more prayerful.[4]

Neglect

As I've sought to grow as a prayerful follower of Jesus and encouraged others in the way of Christ, I've always been intrigued by Jesus' training manual for discipleship which we today call the Sermon on the Mount. Found in the Bible, in chapters 5 – 7 of Matthew's Gospel, Jesus highlights three primary discipleship practices: 'giving' (6:2), 'praying' (6:5) and 'fasting' (6:16). Some Christians today would be surprised to see fasting there, considering it to be a habit for advanced believers or for particularly gifted or spiritually elite people, but Jesus doesn't think so. After all, Jesus doesn't say: '*If* you fast' but '*When* you fast', seeing it as basic to being a believer and part of what some call 'the tripod of discipleship'.[5] German pastor, theologian and martyr Dietrich Bonhoeffer agrees, saying in his famous book *The Cost of Discipleship*, 'Jesus takes it for granted that his disciples will observe the pious custom of fasting.'[6] That means that fasting mustn't be neglected but instead be seen as part of the exciting adventure of discipleship to which all Christ-followers are invited.

I don't consider myself an expert on fasting. I've sometimes been inattentive to this discipline and still feel like something of a novice, recognising that many are more experienced in fasting than me. Having said that, I do fast at various times and for a number of reasons – and I will share some of my thirty-year fasting journey in this book – although I've never engaged in a long fast, so this book will draw on the wisdom of many others. Nevertheless, I've learned that the discipline of fasting is good and important, as I discovered afresh while fasting while writing the bulk of this book during Lent in 2024.[7]

Poverty

Those who understand fasting better than most are people in poverty – those we've traditionally described as 'the poor'. Of course they do, because they often have empty stomachs! They know first-hand what it's like to experience hunger and still be able to survive and even thrive, trusting in God's provision. That's why we need to observe and learn from people in poverty. I have been discovering this in recent years, recognising there's much to learn from those who have little, and that the role of hunger and poverty in fasting is both uncomfortable and yet important. It's the reason why every chapter in this book has something to say about fasting and poverty and how the two interact.

Exempt

I once led a session on fasting with some church leaders. Most said they'd never deliberately fasted by eating nothing. A few tried to explain why fasting really wasn't for them or their church, with one saying that because so many in their community knew hunger due to poverty, it was important that their church fed people rather than encourage fasting. But something about that answer didn't sit well with me, recognising that while feeding the hungry is crucial and something Jesus said disciples should definitely do, he also told them to fast, despite most people in first-century Palestine living in a context of poverty.

I reflected afterwards that when the Bible recommends something difficult that I'm not practising, it's common for me to consider all sorts of reasons why it doesn't apply to me. I know I've done this on a variety of issues over the years, but these days I'm trying to start from a *different* premise, recognising that disciples of Jesus really are called to *follow* him. If Christ is my Master and teacher, then I should approach Scripture positively and aim to do what Jesus does and obey what he says.

Of course, there *may* be particular reasons why a few shouldn't exercise a particular discipline – and with fasting that's usually because of a physical or mental health issue – and if that's the case, then we'll see in this book that there are other fasting-like things that can be done. But most of us *can* fast, and we *should*, because Jesus said so. It's as simple as that. It's a matter of obedience. That doesn't mean it's easy, for the habit will challenge us to think, live and act differently. It requires great vulnerability, deep humility and an honest willingness to change not only our minds but often our well-established habits. To start fasting means we need to be brave and push past the 'not me' mentality, taking lots of small steps into the broader, wider, open landscape of discipleship. The good news is that Jesus promises to give us his Spirit to help us. It's the Holy Spirit who makes fasting not only a duty but a joy; he is key to exercising the habit of fasting for, to use Dallas Willard's helpful phrase, he is 'The Spirit of the Disciplines'.[8]

Mistype

On a lighter note, it might have become apparent to some readers that the word 'fasting' can easily be mistyped – as I've done a number of times when creating this manuscript – resulting in another word with a very different meaning appearing on the page. Spell-checkers can even recommend this word: the word 'farting'! This is not a book about the art of farting, although as you read on you will discover that some partial forms of fasting – like the so-called Daniel Fast (which is basically living on fruit and vegetables for a while) – can have powerful flatulence-inducing effects. I discovered this some years ago when the church I led had a three-week period of fasting where many used the Daniel Fast. Afterwards my wife, Sam, and I reflected that we really should have renamed this time as *21 Days of Prayer and Farting*.

Physical

When we fast, we intentionally make our body hungry so we hunger for God. That's the main reason for Christian fasting. It's more than speaking words, it's using our bodies to pray.

Theologian and pastor Scot McKnight understands this very physical nature of fasting, calling it 'body talk'[9] with his excellent book on fasting having chapters on subjects such as 'Body Turning', 'Body Grief', 'Body Discipline' and

'Body Plea'. As a result I often summarise McKnight's understanding of fasting as 'body prayer', which is a phrase I sometime use when I teach on fasting. This idea that fasting is *body prayer* helps people understand that when we fast our prayers really do become embodied and we *feel* what we pray. The physicality of this kind of praying can rightly be described as *sacramental*, representing an outward sign of an inner reality. Given the avid interest that many today have in using their bodies to express themselves, which is reflected in all kinds of ways from beauty products to gym membership and even tattooing, those who are new to fasting often find this *body prayer* a surprisingly authentic, integrated and physical means of praying.[10]

The chapters of this book pick up this physical idea of *body prayer* and take the reader through a five-stage process of fasting, with each focussing on a different part of the human body. Chapter one understandably starts with the *mouth*, where food enters our body. This is the starting point of fasting: learning to master our mouths and arrest our appetites, so we become intentionally hungry. Chapter two takes us to the *heart*, which is not only the seat of the emotions but the domain of our desires. When we fast our hearts are revealed, our passions exposed and we see what controls us. Chapter three moves to our *hands*, and we get really practical, describing *how* to fast and answering lots of fasting questions in a very hands-on way. In chapter four we focus on our *knees*, observing that fasting is best experienced as a prayerful practice and that we get the most out of it when humbly kneeling in prayer. Finally, chapter five is about our *feet*, recognising that fasting is not just for my personal benefit, making me more healthy or fulfilled; rather, it's for the sake of others. It's meant to impact the way we live in our communities so we can positively impact the world. In short, fasting is a missional practice.

Traditions

So, this book is intentionally very physical. As you read through, you'll discover that each of these five aspects of body-prayer also find a home in a particular tradition of the worldwide church. It fascinates me that the Catholic tradition has especially emphasised the benefits of restricting what we put in our *mouths*. The Orthodox tradition has much to say about our *hearts*, wanting us to exercise self-control so we can steer our passions and perfect our desires. The Anglican tradition, of which I am part, has sought to answer all sorts of practical questions about fasting, wanting us to practise it with our *hands* both helpfully and holistically. The Methodists, especially in their period of growth in the eighteenth and nineteen centuries, stressed the humbling aspects of fasting, inviting Christ-followers to get on their *knees* and pray. And finally, the Pentecostal tradition has shown us how fasting should affect our *feet*, as we seek to walk out our faith as missionary disciples, witnessing to Christ and being his ambassadors in the world. This book will, then, show us how we can learn body-prayer from the richness of God's church.

Dream

Finally, this book on body-prayer feels timely for me to write, as I feel a fresh call to teach and speak about prayerfulness in these present days. Just before I began as a bishop, I had a dream which I later saw as helpfully prophetic in a number of ways. In one part of the dream, I was cleaning out an old fireplace that hadn't been used for a while. I was hoovering up the old embers that had laid cold on the hearth for a long time, preparing things so the fire could be remade and restoked for the coming season. Given that prayer is often linked to fire and is sometimes described as the powerhouse of the church, I interpreted this as a picture of renewed prayer with a restoration of old prayer practices for the present and future context. I know that one of these ancient prayer practices is the habit of fasting. If we could learn to fast again, exercising this powerful practice of body-prayer, then maybe we would see the renewal of God's church and the revival of our nation for which so many of us long and pray. I pray so. I fast so.

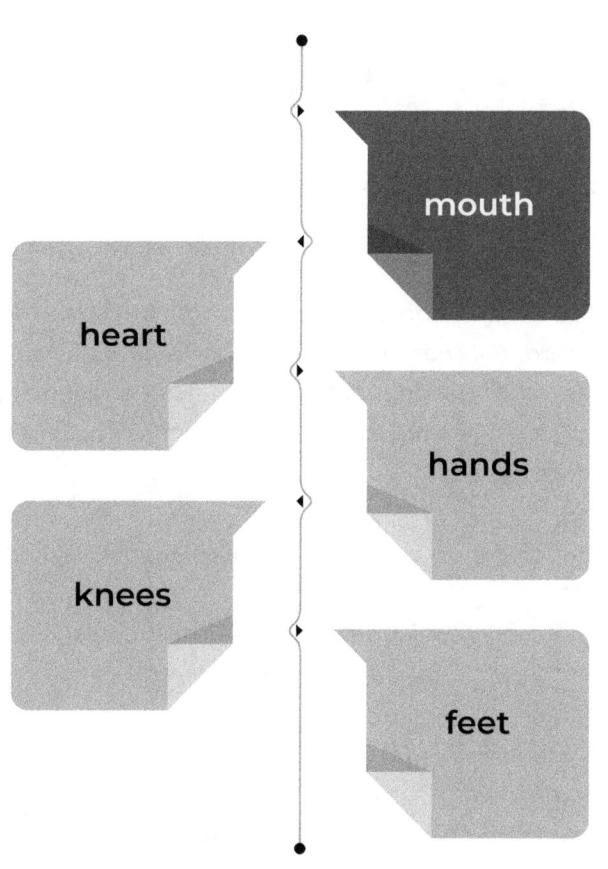

Chapter 1

- *'Jesus ... ate nothing during those days, and at the end of them he was hungry' (Luke 4:2).*

- *'The tempter came to him and said, "If you are the Son of God, tell these stones to become bread." Jesus answered, "It is written: 'Man shall not live on bread alone, but on every word that comes from the mouth of God'"' (Matthew 4:3–4).*

- *'Fasting is ... a bridle of the mouth' (John Chrysostom).*[1]

- *'An empty stomach may be the most powerful prayer posture in Scripture' (Mark Batterson).*[2]

One evening in 1975 an unchurched teenage girl from California heard an evangelist of the Native American Navajo tribe speak passionately about following Jesus. She responded by dedicating her life to Christ, knowing she would never be the same again. While praying some months later the young woman had a vision in which Jesus audibly called her to work in areas of deprivation, and specifically to be a minister and missionary in Asia, England and Africa. The powerful encounter stayed with her so that after marrying a number of years later, she and her husband served in Indonesia and Hong Kong, and then England, before moving to Mozambique in 1995, the poorest country in the world. There they remain to this day, running Bible schools, medical clinics and orphanages, drilling wells, setting up schools, and planting churches. Often seeing miracles and with an expectation of transformation, Heidi and Rolland Baker lead a network of thousands of local churches called Iris, led by indigenous pastors, knowing they're called to serve among people in great poverty.

The Bakers have learned much from those who are poor, especially about hunger. 'What is it about the poor that literally brings the Kingdom of God in a way that the well-fed don't?' asks Heidi. 'It has to do with hunger. It has to do with need. They know they need God. They're hungry and thirsty.'[3] Believing that God wants to feed the hungry and quench the thirsty, the Bakers have learned to seek God in prayer and to ask for his provision in all sorts of ways. As well as helping provide food for people to eat, the Bakers do something that to some might seem counterintuitive: they regularly encourage people in Iris to fast, deliberately restricting what goes into their mouths. 'Fasting does not cause us to gain more favour from God' says Heidi, 'We fast to be more hungry for Him, not to twist His arm.'[4]

The Bakers believe that one of the best ways to learn about fasting is to simply spend time with hungry people. That's why Heidi recommends: 'To learn about hunger, sit with the starving. To learn about thirst, sit with those who have nothing to drink.'[5]

Learning

I used to think I had little or nothing to learn from people in poverty, but having read the Bible I now see things somewhat differently. When Jesus wanted to teach about generosity, he got his disciples to sit near the temple treasury-box and watch, and then when a poor widow with almost nothing gave her last two copper coins, he highlighted *her* as our model for generous giving.[6] As I make clear in *The Art of Giving*: 'We learn about giving money not by observing the rich give, but by watching the poor.'[7] It's the same when it comes to prayer: we learn prayerfulness from observing those in need, especially people in poverty. Many biblical stories of answered prayer are about poor people.[8] This explains why to learn about the power of prayer, the Scriptures invite us to become hungry, identifying with the prayerful poor, through fasting.

Defining

So, what, then, is fasting? A simple definition I've been using for twenty or more years is this: *fasting is choosing not to eat food*. This tells us that:

1. Fasting is about *food*. It's about the food we eat that enables our bodies to survive and thrive. Some extend fasting beyond food to abstaining from other things like negative comments or social media, which can be good and beneficial as we'll discover, especially for those who for health reasons are unable to fast from food, but they're not the same as biblical fasting because they can't generate the physical hunger which comes from food-fasting. Christian fasting is definitely about controlling the *food* we put in our mouths, and we must not assume that fasting from other things is a comparable substitute. It's not.
2. Fasting is about *not eating*. It's about stopping the natural habit of eating. Our bodies say 'feed me' and for a time we say 'no'. As we'll see, many who have learned to control their appetite for food often find they're able to manage all sorts of other appetites too. That's why down the centuries lots of people have found fasting to be a gateway discipline, opening doors to all sorts of other helpful habits.
3. Fasting is about *choosing*. If we don't eat due to illness, or because of famine or incarceration or some other circumstance, that is fasting-like, but it's forced upon us. Christian fasting however, is different; it usually involves choice. We voluntarily decide to fast, choosing to prayerfully partner with the Holy Spirit as we allow ourselves to go hungry.

Twentieth century academic and author C.S. Lewis sometimes fasted in this way. Reflecting on his experience, Lewis later wrote: 'Everyone knows that fasting is a different experience from missing your dinner by accident or through poverty. Fasting asserts the will against the appetite – the reward being self-mastery and the danger pride.'[9] It's interesting that Lewis knew that for all its good, there is, as in every habit, a dark side to fasting. US pastor John Piper agrees, so much so that the very first words of his book on fasting read: 'Beware of books on fasting'![10] That's why I want to be honest about my fasting journey in this book. When I first started fasting, it was tempting to want to give myself some kind of badge of merit. We're all tempted to do this, even wanting to show off and tell people how well we're doing, in the hope of approval and honour. Jesus understood this, recognising that it's common to fast with impure motives, so when he first teaches on fasting in Matthew 6, the majority of Jesus' guidance is about how *not* to fast, saying:

> When you fast, do not look sombre as the hypocrites do, for they disfigure their faces to show others they are fasting . . . But when you fast, put oil on your head and wash your face, so that it will not be obvious to others . . .
>
> *Matthew 6:16–18*

Jesus is not saying that fasting should be highly secretive but rather that his followers should check their attitude and not show off. So, if fasting is not to display discipline to others, why do it? The answer is so obvious that it took me a while to grasp it in its glorious simplicity: fasting is about becoming hungry; it's about intentionally starving your body.

Eating

Like most people, I like eating. I enjoy my food and appreciate that contented after-dinner sense of feeling full. Conversely, I don't like feeling hungry. Having an empty stomach is not a pleasant sensation, and it's not supposed to be. Hunger is meant to make us feel uncomfortable, for it's the body's natural way of saying 'feed me' with more calories. The word *calorie* is commonly used as shorthand for kilocalorie, which is a measure of energy contained in food and drink. According to advice from the United Kingdom's National Health Service, 'The ideal daily intake of calories varies depending on age, metabolism and levels of physical activity, among other things. Generally, the recommended daily calorie intake is 2,000 calories a day for women and 2,500 for men.'[11] We get most of these calories from eating food.

The Christian Scriptures, from beginning to end, are very positive about eating food. The very first chapter of the Bible, in Genesis 1 describes God creating an abundant world full of multiplying life, much of which is given 'for food' (Genesis 1:29,30), and the final chapters of Revelation describe heaven as a wedding (Revelation 21) which in

Jewish culture always involved food, and as a place where there is a 'tree of life', bearing much fruit (22:2) in which we're invited to share (22:14,19).[12] Consuming food in Near Eastern culture in biblical times enabled humans to live and grow, but it also had a social function in the family and community, as people ate together and shared kindness, friendship and hospitality. Family events usually involved food, as did community gatherings and religious festivals. If a guest came, you always fed them. Much of Jewish worship described in the Old Testament involved sacrificing the 'firstfruits'[13] of food products, both as an act of thanksgiving as well as trust, trusting that the remainder of the harvest would be sufficient. In the New Testament we often read of Jesus eating with people, especially those who were social outcasts, so much so that his critics mocked him as 'a glutton and a drunkard'.[14] Before his sacrificial death, it's notable that Jesus chose to eat with his followers – what we now call the Last Supper – and he was clear that he would not eat again until after his death. He also told his followers to share bread and wine as a continual memory of his sacrificial death.[15] In summary, the Christian Scriptures value eating, seeing food as a God-given gift to be enjoyed and shared.

Given this positivity about food, I've been surprised to discover that the church down the ages has had a mixed attitude towards eating, with many being wary of over-indulging.[16]

There are a variety of reasons for this. One is that Jesus sometimes fasted and assumed his followers would do the same, causing some to be reluctant to encourage too much feasting. Another factor is that the early church fathers were critical of over-eating. Living in the first four centuries after Christ, the fathers not only urged Christians to share food with people in poverty, but they also saw human physical desires as pointing to the greater, spiritual desire for union with Christ to be fulfilled in eternity. As a result, many urged self-control on all physical pleasures, especially the desire to eat. Restraint was paramount with Basil the Great (AD 330–379), for example, teaching that the stomach should not be full, and that eating should be for necessity and not for pleasure. Monks should eat as little as possible to get by, and be satisfied with water to drink.[17]

Today in the twenty-first century, lots of churches, especially in the West, have a different attitude to eating, recognising the important role that food can play in creating community. Eating together after worship or midweek in small groups is central to the communal life of many churches that I've been part of, affirming the place of corporate celebration and thanksgiving, often based around eating. In recent years lots of UK churches have established foodbanks and community groceries, realising that many struggle to afford food to feed themselves and their family. Food has also had an impact on the church's evangelism. The Alpha course, for example, is built around eating while considering questions of faith, which has had a huge impact on the attitude to the church in the UK to food and evangelism.[18]

One result of all this positivity about eating, however, is that many churches have neglected the discipline of fasting. They've found it difficult to encourage both eating *and* not eating. But both we *must* do, for if we step back and look at Scripture as a whole, we see that the Bible is positive about both feasting *and* fasting. It's not either/or, it's both/and. The two rightly belong together, as Christ showed us.

Jesus
Jesus helps us understand the importance of both feasting *and* of fasting, for he practised both and wants his church to do the same. Jesus wants us to be full: full of life and love, goodness and generosity. Full of his Spirit. Full to overflowing, so we can share with others. We celebrate that through feasting on food, and as result we feel full. But Christ also wants us to be empty: empty of sin and selfishness, pride and pomposity. Empty of evil. Empty of ungodly ambitions and aspirations, so we can be open to God's greater and higher agenda. We celebrate that through fasting of food, and as a result we feel hungry.

As I began to see this, I came to realise that hunger can be a surprising means through which Christ teaches me so much. When hungry I've learned what it is to be weak. When hungry I've learned what it is to lack. When hungry I've learned what it is to be reliant. It's when I'm hungry that I've understood so much about myself, about people in poverty and about God. These are the hunger-themes that will be explored in the remainder of this first chapter, showing why it's important from time to time to get hungry by controlling what I put in my mouth.

Weak

Like most people, when I don't eat it takes just a few hours for hunger pangs to come and for my body to feel weak, so I normally find some food and eat. This cycle of eating shows me something I find uncomfortable to consider: that I'm fundamentally fragile. Eating just masks it, but not for very long. Fasting has therefore helped me recognise my inherent weakness as a human being, which is both troubling yet true.

We all start off life weak, weak as a baby, and we end up weak, as our bodies age and become tired and frail. Even the period in-between, when our bodies are in their prime and at their strongest, we aren't able to do everything we want. We have physical, intellectual and emotional limits. So, if we work too hard or too long, we burn out. That's why we need to slow down. To get some sleep. To take at least one weekly rest-day and regular seasons when we change our pace. And in particular we need others. We need their help, their abilities, their wisdom and their kindness, so together we can make up for our weaknesses and be a team. This is what families are all about. And workplace teams. And churches. And communities. And nations. We need each other, because on our own we are weak. Weakness is intrinsic to what it is to be a human being.

Being told that we're weak is, for some, a rather unpalatable message to chew on, but it's a reality that we'd do well to recognise, and one of the best ways to do this is to fast. Don't put food in your mouth for just a few hours or days, and notice how you feel. You'll soon come face to face with your human weakness. Many aren't willing to even try, but what if you did? What if instead of eating or snacking you explored the hunger, seeking to learn from it and mature through it? What would happen? Most people in the West have no idea, as other than being ill they've never been hungry. Unless they've experienced poverty most have never experienced the physical weakness that comes from hunger. Unless they've fasted. For fasting is about deliberately making your body weak. When we do that, all sorts of fascinating things happen.

Detox

One thing that can occur when we fast is that our physical and mental health improves. The BBC's respected *Good*

Food website, for example, lists ten potential benefits from making your body weak through fasting, saying that fasting:

- **supports hormones and genes that influence metabolism.** When fasting your body adapts via a change in hormone levels, accessing stored body fat and initiating repair processes;
- **may support weight loss.** Undertaking short-term fasts may aid weight reduction, fat loss and improve blood lipids;
- **supports blood sugar management.** Several studies support fasting as a means of improving blood sugar control and potentially reducing the risk of diabetes, although gender may play a part. There can also be benefits for those with Type 2 Diabetes, decreasing fasting glucose and fasting insulin, reducing insulin resistance and decreasing leptin;
- **supports gut health.** Fasting can improve the diversity and number of beneficial bacteria in the gut, aiding weight change, waist measurement and metabolism;
- **supports heart health.** Studies suggest it may reduce some of the risk factors for heart disease, including blood pressure, cholesterol and markers of inflammation;
- **may help disease prevention.** When we fast, the body initiates a process called autophagy, when waste materials from cells are removed, enabling

the body to better manage chronic inflammation and reducing the risk of conditions such as heart disease, multiple sclerosis and rheumatoid arthritis;

- **may delay ageing and support growth and metabolism.** Fasting, and adopting a diet low in protein may extend life. It appears to promote levels of human growth hormone, which aids repair, metabolism, weight loss, muscle strength and exercise performance. Current longevity research is largely limited to animals, so more studies are needed;
- **may reset your circadian rhythm.** Fasting changes in the levels of chemicals called metabolites that act as signalling molecules to our central body clock. In this way, fasting may help reset our circadian (24 hour) rhythm and benefit conditions like obesity that are associated with a disordered body clock;
- **may support brain function.** Animal studies suggest fasting may protect against and improve outcomes in Parkinson's and Alzheimer's, as well as stimulate brain function by supporting memory and brain processing and the production of nerve cells;
- **may reduce anxiety.** Human studies report fasting may reduce symptoms of anxiety and depression and improve social connection. Again, more studies are needed.[19]

So, making myself temporarily weak through fasting can give my body a detox, helping renew a variety of organs and bodily functions, and enabling me to think more clearly and live better. These surprising benefits are available to all through fasting, which explains why some people, even if they have no religion, choose to fast. Also, there's the slimming side-effect too, which I would argue is not a great motive for fasting, for if you want to lose weight, just go on a diet!

While my body will experience short-term weakness though fasting, as long as I'm careful in the manner and length of fasting, it will not become damaged. When Heidi Baker's mother heard she had become a follower of Jesus and had begun to fast occasionally she was horrified. Heidi said, 'She thought I was going to die if I didn't eat something.'[20] Many who have never fasted think this. They don't understand the benefits of intentionally making your body weak.

Catholicism
As well as physical benefits, there are prayer benefits too. In today's Western world such things are often overlooked or dismissed, but they are important and are at the heart of fasting for people of faith and especially for followers of Jesus, who don't primarily fast for physical reasons, but for its devotional benefits. One tradition of the church that has especially emphasised this is Roman Catholicism.

The Roman Catholic Church has always had a strong emphasis on disciplines, particularly linking them to an annual rhythm of worship called 'the liturgical calendar'. Each of the four seasons are begun with fasting on so-called Ember Days, although the most important fasting period is the forty days running up to Easter, known as Lent, where worshippers are expected to fast during the morning hours before receiving Holy Communion. In addition, fasting has always been encouraged on Fridays. The purpose of this is to produce hunger in order to master our sinful human nature that so often expresses itself in a lack of discipline in a variety of bodily desires, especially for food and sex which, when unboundaried, can easily lead to gluttony and sexual immorality. Catholicism teaches that fasting helps us redirect these basic appetites in order to use them well and creatively. That's why, when it comes to fasting, Thomas Aquinas said that fasting had three main purposes: 'First, in order to bridle the lusts of the flesh . . . Secondly in order that the mind may more freely contemplate heavenly things . . . Thirdly, in order to satisfy for sins.'[21] This penitential side of fasting has been especially strong in the Catholic tradition, recognising fasting's ability to suppress and channel innate desires. Various studies support this, as does my own lived experience, noticing my libido often decreasing when fasting. St Cyril of Jerusalem spoke of this, saying: 'So, let us keep a check on our stomach, in order to keep a check on that which is below the stomach.'[22] It's notable that since the Vatican II Council of the 1960s, led by Pope John XXIII, fasting has become a *voluntary* practice for Catholics, to the criticism of some who see fasting as a foundational Catholic discipline that is now disappearing. This change in emphasis partly reflects the Catholic Church's desire to see the hunger and weakness produced by fasting as a positive invitation to grace, rather than just a negative renunciation of sin.

Delight

The apostle Paul understood that becoming weak through hunger had positive benefits, writing in his second letter to the Corinthians: 'I will boast all the more gladly about my weaknesses, so that Christ's power may rest on me.' As he continued to reflect on this he even said, 'I delight in weaknesses.' Why? 'For when I am weak, then I am strong.'[23] It seems that Paul found a surprising source of strength discovered in weakness. Contemporary author and teacher Dallas Willard thinks this happens especially through spiritual disciplines, saying that: 'The need for extensive practice of a given discipline is an indication of our *weakness*, not our strength.'[24] Willard considers the best prayer discipline to empower us in our weakness is the habit of fasting. 'Since food has the pervasive place it does in our lives,' says Willard, 'the effects of fasting will be diffused throughout our lives.'[25]

At first, I wasn't sure about this, but now, having fasted in various forms over a number of years, I agree. I know fasting makes me weak, which means that I can sometimes be reluctant to get started, but once I do there are always benefits. It's rather like when I go swimming in the sea. As someone who doesn't like cold water, I normally take a while to get in and under, having to suppress my initial reluctance. But once I'm in I'm fine – and I know that what I'm doing is good. Fasting is rather like that. I often have to push myself to get started, but when I do and begin to feel hungry and call on God for strength, I find surprising resources, fortifying not just my body but my heart and mind and will. It feels like the Lord honours the vulnerability and weakness of fasting.

The person who models this weakness best however is not Paul; it's Jesus Christ. Christ is the One who in his incarnation became weak, being born as a vulnerable baby, taking on frail humanity, and dying a humiliating slave's death by crucifixion, experiencing the slow draining away of all the juices of life from his naked, broken torso. While inhabiting his weak body, Jesus emptied himself of any personal agenda,[26] saying his desire was 'not to do my will but . . . the will of him who sent me'.[27] Yet in his weakness Christ found strength, for as he particularly affirmed his identification with weak and sinful humanity at his baptism, so God's strong Spirit descended upon him,[28] and most particularly as he sacrificed his weak body on the cross, so forgiveness and freedom, grace and glory were powerfully released. This salvation – this powerful liberty – won for us by Christ was achieved in weakness. This means when I fast not only am I granted a heightened experience of the intrinsic weakness of being human, but I also identify with the human weakness Christ experienced, and recognise that it's in weakness that God reveals his strength.

This is surely why Paul is able to say he 'delights' in weakness, and others agree, including Catholic monk Adalbert de Vogüé, who said that the more he fasted it 'was no longer a constraint and penance for me, but a joy and need of body and soul. I practiced it spontaneously because I loved it.'[29]

Chris and Nora emailed me recently, having discovered something of this delight in fasting, saying:

Whilst we've been fasting we've been making Jesus a priority, which has improved our prayer life. Discovering new ways of praying (i.e. contemplatively, liturgy, praying through Psalms etc.) has turned a practice that had become somewhat monotonous into something we look forward to doing. As we have done this, we've felt God's closeness in both the good and the more challenging parts of life.

Lack

The first time I fasted and my body began to feel weak through hunger, I couldn't stop thinking that this is how many poor people have felt throughout history. Most people who fast think this, realising that experiencing hunger is the common condition of those who don't have enough to eat, and they feel a strangely compelling association with them. This is part of what happens when we fast, and *it's how it's meant to be*. We share in the pain of the world. This is the world full of abundant resources, where despite the rising world population experts say there's still more than enough food for everyone, and yet many people still go hungry. Our world feels like it lacks, and as we fast we recognise in a very real way that this is the lived experience of many: they don't have enough food and they're hungry.

Down the ages and still today, scarcity is the normal condition for lots of people. As we fast and understand how it feels to experience insufficiency, it's common for us to want to help those who lack. We feel compassion. We want to care, provide and resource. For Christ-followers like me, who ask God each day to 'give us today our daily bread',[30] this is a challenge not just to pray this prayer for myself but for *others* too, and then to go further: to turn my prayers into action and be part of the answer to that prayer with practical aid for people in poverty.

Care

Followers of Jesus have often been at the forefront of social care, concerned to respond to human need by loving service and to transform unjust structures of society, to challenge violence of every kind and pursue peace and reconciliation.[31] Many historians, including Rodney Stark[32] and Alan Kreider,[33] have shown that the growth of the church in the first few centuries of its existence was caused mainly through practical care given to those in need. Christ-followers particularly supported widows and orphans, the two poorest and most vulnerable social groups, who were often most neglected by wider society. Throughout history and across cultures it's often been Christians who've established hospitals for the sick, schools for children and hospices for the dying, with evidence showing that communities who fast often have a special concern for those in need, for true fasting should release a fresh wave of care for people in poverty and those experiencing injustice. Indeed if it doesn't, there's something very wrong, as the prophet Isaiah realises, saying in 58:6–7:

> Is not this the kind of fasting I have chosen:
> to loose the chains of injustice
> and untie the cords of the yoke,
> to set the oppressed free
> and break every yoke?
> Is it not to share your food with the hungry

and to provide the poor wanderer with shelter –
when you see the naked, to clothe them,
and not to turn away from your own flesh and blood?

These powerful prophetic words show that fasting without caring for people in need not only lacks integrity but is not recognised by God as genuine fasting. Early church father Clement of Alexandria (AD 155–220) knew this, referencing Isaiah 58 when discussing fasting, and teaching that truly good deeds must be prioritised above ritual.[34] To fast without compassion for those in need is not effective fasting, for it hasn't changed our hearts. Isaiah 58 could not be clearer on this. Making our bodies hungry through fasting is meant to cause us to be more compassionate and caring, as we identify with people in poverty, sharing in their hunger.

This deep identification with the poor was so important to the church in its early years that the second-century Athenian Christian philosopher Aristedes explained that one of the main Christian motives for fasting was to take the food you would have eaten and give it to people in poverty, saying: 'And if there is among them any that is poor and needy, and if they have no spare food, they fast two or three days in order to supply to the needy their lack of food.'[35] Similarly the Shepherd of Hermas, writing at a similar time in Rome, said, 'having reckoned up the price of the dishes of that day which you intended to have eaten, you will give it to a widow, or an orphan, or to some person in want.'[36] Origen of Alexandria (AD 185–253) agreed, declaring: 'For in a certain book we find this saying by the apostles: "Blessed is one who also fasts that he may feed the poor."'[37] When I first read these statements about fasting I was deeply challenged, realising that I'd fasted many times but never linked it to supporting people in poverty, yet the premise is so simple: *fast, and give to the poor the money saved by not eating*. Imagine how homeless people and social care charities would benefit if followers of Jesus did this, again and again? All this means that fasting is not just to help me identify with people in poverty, but to spur me to support them.

Reliant

People in poverty have little. They struggle to have sufficient shelter, clothing and food, and often go hungry. They know they're reliant on others: on people and God. I've observed this as I've spent time in places like Burundi, in East Africa, one of the poorest countries on the planet, and seen the vibrant worship and humble prayer of these precious, often hungry people. They know they need help and they regularly find themselves crying out to the Lord for food to alleviate their hunger. As they do this, they often discover something significant: that even if their bodies are hungry, the Lord feeds their souls.

God loves to give life-giving bread to hungry people. He has food available to all in need, who are humble and vulnerable enough to come and ask. People in poverty have often discovered this through their physical hunger. Those in affluence may never find this until their life falls apart, or unless they make themselves deliberately hungry through fasting. When I fast in this way, here's what I've found: *Christ satisfies.* It is not without reason that Jesus says, 'I am the bread of life. Whoever comes to me will never go hungry, and whoever believes in me will never be thirsty.'[38] When fasting I discover delicious delights in tasting the bread of life. As I feast on Christ especially through Spirit, Scripture and sacrament, I find the satisfaction of such nourishment to be surprisingly enhanced through fasting.

Feast

'Fasting', says Dallas Willard, 'confirms our utter dependence upon God by finding in him a source of sustenance beyond food.'[39] Lou Engle, who for forty or more years has been encouraging the American church to prayerfully fast agrees, saying: 'I have a love-hate relationship with fasting because, in fasting, I actually feast on God. This is really what happens. I deny myself the legitimate pleasures of food for the supreme pleasures of knowing God and of encountering Him. Fasting in His grace has literally always put the fire back in my heart.'[40] I have found this, as I've fasted while writing this book on fasting. Taking time not just to study, reflect and write but to do so *in the context of fasting* is restoring joy to my weary soul and a love for the Lord and for people. I can sense it, in my attitude to people I am meeting and in my prayers.

When I was vicar of The Belfrey in York, we sometimes had seasons of fasting. During one in Lent 2023, we encouraged those who could to fast on Wednesdays and then to meet in the evening for corporate prayer, followed by a shared meal to break the fast. We wanted to model Christ's call for us to be people who both fast *and* feast and to do so *together* for, as we'll see, there is power in fasting and more still in *corporate* fasting. But looking back I think I failed to adequately explain that the fasting itself can be feasting. Spending focussed time in prayer with Jesus, with bodies feeling weak and hungry, can be notably nourishing. Like a mouth-watering meal, we sumptuously sup on Christ. This partly explains what Jesus has in mind when he is asked about fasting in Matthew 9:14–15. Here's the story:

> Then John's disciples came and asked him, 'How is it that we and the Pharisees fast often, but your disciples do not fast?' Jesus answered, 'How can the guests of the bridegroom mourn while he is with them? The time will come when the bridegroom will be taken from them; then they will fast.'

It seems that despite Christ telling his disciples to fast, that they didn't practise the discipline during Jesus' public ministry as much as some others. Given what's been positively said so far about fasting in this book, that might come as a surprise, with these verses from Matthew 9 hard to reconcile. So how should we understand this, and what does it means for our fasting today? Jesus explains by describing himself as like the bridegroom at a wedding. In the Jewish culture of Jesus' day, weddings were marked by food and festivity, and funerals by fasting and mourning. So, says Jesus, when he's physically present with them it's like 'wedding time': it's a time to eat and party, and enjoy the kingdom of God which Jesus both brings and embodies. As his disciples are with him in his presence, they are feasting. But, referring to his death and then his return to heaven, Jesus says there will come a time when 'the bridegroom will be taken from them'. That's the era in which we presently live – between the two comings of Christ – which is the time to fast. This means I fast partly as a physical act of mourning, sad that Jesus is not physically present with us, but I also fast as a spiritual act of feasting, recognising that Christ *is* present by his Spirit, and despite his physical absence he is known and experienced. We do not see him 'fully' but, as Paul says to the Corinthians, 'through a glass, darkly'.[41] I know him, but there is more to know. I will 'fully' experience him in heaven, encountering him in all his glory, at which time there'll be no need to fast.

Joy

This paradox between Christ being present but not fully so, reflects what theologians call 'the eschatological tension' between the *now* and *not yet* of God's kingdom. When Christ walked this earth he brought God's kingdom wherever he went. What joy! When he returns, or when our bodies die and we join him in eternity, we'll experience this kingdom in all its bounty. Again, what joy! Now, in these in-between days, we experience God's kingdom in part. We know partial joy!

In this place of partial joy, I've been learning that I'm called to prayerfulness, praying and working to see more of this kingdom of goodness here on earth as in heaven. These are *in-between days* when I both eat and don't eat. I feast and fast. But I mustn't forget that even the fasting can be a time of feasting, if I come to Christ in my hunger and dine! Indeed, Jesus has food for us to eat that's only tasted when we fast. Encountering Jesus in a fresh way is surely one of the 'rewards' of fasting that Jesus talks about in Matthew 6:18, which are not earned but naturally flow from the grace that we receive from tasting and seeing that 'the LORD is good'.[42] The way to do this is simple: by becoming hungry.

My elderly mother, Christine Porter, tasted something of this during a time of fasting that took place at The Belfrey in York in 2017. The church family was encouraged to fast for encounter, praying for friends and family who did not yet know Christ to experience him, and also for fresh encounters for Christ-followers too. During this time my mother, who for age and health reasons was not fasting, told me that when praying one day during this time, she experienced the presence of Jesus like never before in her eighty years of life. It was lovely, deep and moving, renewing her heart. At the end of the fast, and with her permission, I mentioned this in a sermon, going on to say, 'Maybe you were someone who fasted in this season and didn't have a particular encounter with Christ for yourself. But maybe your fasting helped someone else, like my mother. If that was you, thank you.' Afterwards a few people came up to me and said they had always considered fasting a practice for their own benefit, and didn't realise it could help someone else. But it can.

So having seen in this chapter that fasting is about hunger and being disciplined about what we eat through our *mouths,* so we next consider what this does for our *hearts*. This is the main difference between secular and sacred fasting. Secular fasting is purely for its physical benefits, while sacred fasting recognises that its benefits are so much broader and more expansive, if we're willing to change by opening our hearts.

- fasting is choosing not to eat food
- fasting is about becoming hungry
- fasting is particularly learned by spending time with people in poverty
- fasting teaches us to rely on God
- fasting is an invitation to feast on Christ

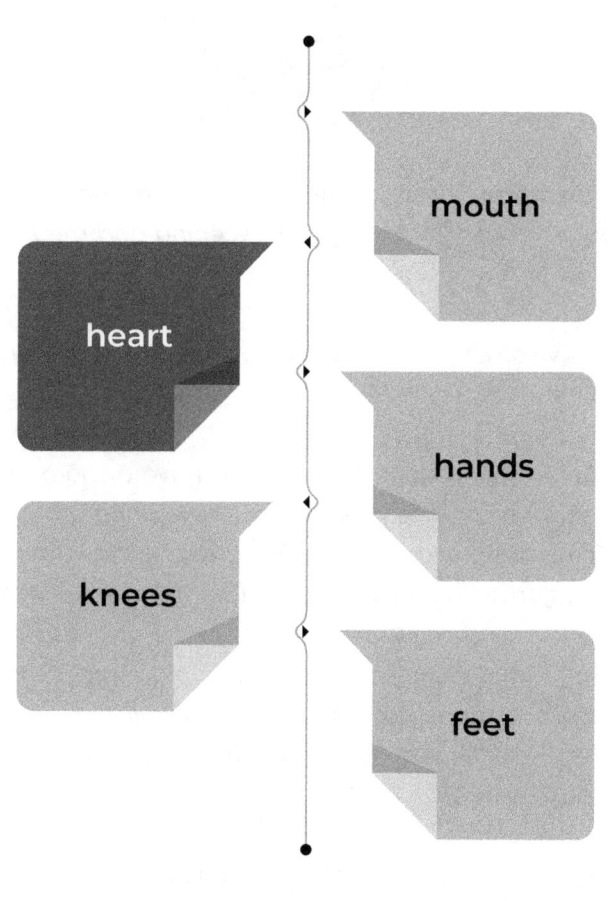

Chapter 2

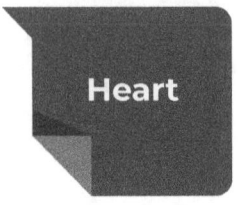

- *'"Even now," declares the LORD, "return to me with all your heart, with fasting and weeping and mourning"' (Joel 2:12).*

- *'Above all else, guard your heart, for it is the well-spring of life' (Proverbs 4:23).*

- *'If our fasting doesn't lead us to have a more tender heart, respond more swiftly to the leading of the Holy Spirit, move with compassion, love the lost, give to the needy, then we are not doing it right' (Jennifer Miskov).*[1]

- *'Spiritual disciplines such as fasting are practices and habits that orientate our hearts and minds to see past the distractions of our culture and uncover the heart of God' (David Docusen).*[2]

Friday 6th of February 1756 was certainly a day for picking up a pen to write. It was 'a glorious day' according to one man, who as night descended reflected on the day's events by scribbling in his notebook. The man was not unused to journal-writing, often recording his reflections, interesting thoughts and comments and sometimes even his prayers. Like all English people of the time, he was concerned about the nation's arch-enemy, the kingdom of France, who was preparing to cross the Channel for a land invasion. Such an event had not occurred in England for nearly seven hundred years since the time of William the Conqueror, but all knew imminent invasion was likely. The military were preparing defences on the south coast, and Members of Parliament at Westminster were debating the matter with concern, worried for the nation's future. King George II shared parliament's apprehension and so the king made the strategic step of calling his English people to action: inviting them not to take up swords or ploughshares but to take up their Bibles and prayer books, for a day of prayer and fasting.

The journal-writer was a prominent itinerant preacher. He was in London for the day, not to preach but to join with others in prayer. Being someone of devotional disposition, known for his disciplined life which he learned from the church fathers who had especially shaped the Orthodox Church, the preacher gladly joined the fast, asking the Lord to stay the hand of the enemy. As he walked the streets, he visited a number of churches and observed people in prayer, calling out to God for mercy. 'Every church in the city was more than full' he wrote that evening, 'and a solemn seriousness sat on every face'. Now at the end of the day he had a strong conviction not just that the nation's prayers had been heard, but that they had been answered, for his journal-entry ended by his penning these words of faithful expectation: 'Surely God heareth the prayer, and there will yet be a lengthening of our tranquility.' And there was, for many days later the journal-writer, John Wesley, added a footnote which read: 'Humility was turned into national rejoicing for the threatened invasion by the French was averted.'[3] To date, still no land invasion has occurred on our isles for nearly a thousand years.

Days of prayer and fasting have taken place throughout history in many nations, not just in England. Leaders have invited people not only to pray, but also to fast. To not eat. To make their bodies uncomfortably hungry while praying. Such acts of vulnerability were undertaken in the belief that it would aid their prayers, showing purpose and passion to the God who ultimately controlled their history and destiny. Reflecting an attitude of humility and a desire for divine help, their fasting was part of a desperate heart-cry to God. It is this heart-response and heart-desire behind all true fasting that is the theme of this second chapter.

This chapter considers the intent of fasting, which is not just to empty the stomach and become hungry, but to empty the heart and become humble. Fasting is supposed to reflect a lowly disposition and a desire for our souls to be renewed. The prophet Joel speaks in God's name of this, declaring: 'return to me with all your heart, with fasting and weeping and mourning.'[4] This was not just a call to pray, but to do so with energy, enthusiasm and emotion – *with all their heart*.

Desires

In most cultures when they speak of the heart, they don't mean the important engine-like organ that pumps blood around our bodies, rather they mean the centre of their being. The heart is often viewed as the seat of our feelings, with expert on emotions and shame Brené Brown describing the heart as 'the universal metaphor for our capacity to love and be loved, and it's the symbolic gateway to our emotional lives'.[5] As well as the emotional core, the heart is also seen as the centre of our *desires*, with the Psalms speaking of the longings of our hearts.[6] These desires might be good and virtuous, but they could be selfish and sinful, or a mix. Scripture teaches that God understands this, observing the wants, hopes and motives of our hearts, with 1 Samuel 16:7 saying that 'People look at the outward appearance, but the LORD looks at the heart.' This means that God sees us and reads us and knows our desires better than we do. Where our hearts are impure, he wants to forgive and change them.[7]

According to philosopher James K.A. Smith, to have a virtuous heart requires us to develop 'good moral habits'.[8] For Smith, this requires deliberate training, because 'virtues are learned and acquired, through imitation and practice'. They don't come naturally, but rather are like 'moral muscles that are trained in the same way our biological muscles are trained when we practice a golf swing or piano scales'.[9] This means that habit formation is central to the reorientation of our hearts, and one of the most helpful habits that transforms our hearts is the discipline of fasting.

Johannes Hartl is the Catholic leader of the Augsburg House of Prayer in Germany and has good experience of individual and corporate fasting. Understanding its central role in virtue-formation, he says with simple clarity: 'The point of a lifestyle characterised by fasting and prayer is not to prove to God just how serious I am, but that it changes my heart.'[10] All this was expressed well to me in an email I received in 2019:

September 2019

Hi Matthew,

I have tried fasting ages ago when I was a relatively new Christian (with some success but on a very limited scale!)

but not really engaged with it since, other than sometimes skipping lunch when it's convenient, rather than to better meet with God. I was really struck by Isaiah 58, v 8 during x's sermon: 'Then your light will break forth like the dawn, and your healing will quickly appear; then your righteousness will go before you, and the glory of the LORD will be your rear guard.' I kept reading this verse [and sensed God was speaking to me about] freedom from comfort eating . . .

While on holiday recently I had a bit of an 'epiphany' where I knew God was working in me and unearthing some things, but hadn't realised quite how much or what. I ended up (inadvertently at first) fasting lunch most days (unheard of for me while away as I like to eat and was on holiday!) and then spending lots of time praying and with God, in worship or just quietly. I realised on my return (once back home alone, when things could have reverted to how they had been before I left), that I have been completely freed, at least for the time being – I'm hoping it's permanent! – of the need to comfort eat or overeat the wrong things. I'm enjoying food like never before and also just so grateful for the newfound freedom God has released me in to, in all sorts of other areas of my life too . . .

God bless you and thank you,

Maria

For Maria, fasting exposed a desire to comfort eat, causing her to initiate heart-change.

Holiness

This renewal of the heart is about what the saints of old called growing in holiness. Holiness is becoming more God-like and is best realised by observing Jesus, who is 'the Holy One',[11] and by living in relationship with him. Twentieth century Anglican leader and author John Stott recognised this, helpfully saying: 'holiness is Christlikeness, and Christlikeness is God's eternal purpose for his children.'[12]

What does this mean for the hearts of disciples of Jesus who, as we've been learning, are invited to develop discipleship habits, such as fasting? It means that holiness is our aim. It's our character goal. It means that having a holy heart is my desire, as I tell myself and God that I want to become more Christ-like. While this side of heaven there will always be more maturing required, holiness is nevertheless my aim. It also means that I need all the help I can get to become more holy, including embracing all the holy habits available. St Basil believed the most important was fasting, saying: 'in general you will find that fasting guided all the saints to a godly way of life.'[13] This is why John Piper warns: 'Woe to fasting that leaves sin in our lives untouched.'[14] So how do we become more virtuous and holy in heart, through fasting?

Orthodoxy

While all traditions of the church emphasise the heart-change that comes through fasting, this has been a particularly strong emphasis of the Orthodox Church. Rooted in the teaching of the fathers of the first four centuries of the church, Orthodoxy has always taught that fasting from food is intrinsic to Christian discipleship, teaching two types of fasting: *normal* fasting and *ascetic* fasting. Normal fasting is required on Wednesdays and Friday and in preparation for receiving the Eucharist. It is also practised vigorously in the forty-day period running up to Easter which they call 'The Great Lent', and also in Advent, the forty days prior to Christmas which they call 'The Nativity Fast'. They also fast on other holy days, recognising that hunger produces expectation and anticipation, refocussing the passions and desires in our hearts. This has always been important in Orthodoxy, with Basil the Great saying, 'you who are about to fast should not look gloomy . . . but beautify yourself in accordance with the gospel, not despondent over the emptiness of your stomach but rather delighting in your soul because of the spiritual joys.'[15] This reflects the eschatological gladness of God's kingdom that we saw in chapter one, which we experience in some measure now and will be fully realised in eternity. Fasting can help us experience something of this kingdom, causing our passions to be redirected and our hearts transformed. Rather than emphasising the negative subjugation of our sinful nature which fasting can produce, Orthodoxy is a rich tradition that especially values the positive transformation that fasting creates in our hearts, producing hopeful joy and festive delight as our desires are transformed.

Recalibration

When I fast, I've discovered that a number of things happen in my heart that begin to shape these desires. In the same way that an instrument such as a clock, or compass, or pump is serviced and recalibrated in order to function properly, so through fasting my heart receives needful maintenance and recalibration, so it can function as God intends.

Here are five ways I've found this heart-recalibration can happen through fasting.

1. Conviction

First, heart-change happens when fasting through humble *conviction*.

When I fast, I notice things, especially things about my desires. For those new to fasting, this can be surprising and even unwelcome, as fasting sometimes exposes not only virtuous things of which we want to see more, but hidden sinful yearnings of which we want to see less. The Spirit of God does this not to shame us but to change us, wanting to lovingly form us increasingly into the likeness of Christ,[16] so our lives display more of what Paul in Galatians 5:22 calls 'the fruit of the [Holy] Spirit'. Fourth-century Archbishop of Constantinople John Chrysostom understood this, teaching that 'the honour of fasting consists not in abstinence from food, but in withdrawing from sinful practices'.[17] Sometimes when I've fasted a past sinful action or selfish habit has come to mind; I know I've done wrong and change is needed. Occasionally when fasting my mind has replayed an event that at the time seemed fine but as I consider it again I see things with new perspective, now recognising how my comments or actions hurt others or my motives were impure. This is the holy power of prayerful fasting in the presence of the Holy Spirit.

Some find that when they fast the Spirit particularly shows them things that have power over them. These could be unhealthy patterns or habits that have become addictions, perhaps in areas such as money and spending; alcohol and stimulants; sex and unhealthy relationships. Writer on spiritual disciplines Richard Foster expresses it like this: 'More than any other discipline, fasting reveals the things that control us. This is a wonderful benefit to the true disciple.'[18]

This conviction often impacts our aspirations. For example, I know people who've told me that when they've prayerfully fasted, not only have they recognised they need to be more generous, but their financial goals have changed. No longer is being financially comfortable their main aim, now they want to resource God's kingdom, and especially help people in poverty as they identify with them through fasting. Other ambitions may be transformed too. A desire for an easy life might be changed into a desire for an impactful life. A dream to be famous might be morphed into a desire to make Christ famous. A yearning for love might be changed into a passion to love others.

These purified desires come as we welcome the convicting presence of the Spirit, whose work in our life is sometimes described in refining terms, rather like a silver or goldsmith who stirs hot metal in a crucible in order to produce the purest product from the alloy. This is why many down the centuries have described fasting in fiery terms. Jennifer Miskov has noticed this, saying, 'Fasting and fire are inseparable. There is something about fasting that ignites an all-consuming fire for God inside.'[19] The Orthodox Church teaches that the angels of God love this and are often sent by God to assist this fiery work of repentance. After all, one of the names given to angels in Hebrew 1:7 is 'flames of fire'.[20] We see this in Isaiah 6:1–7, when the prophet Isaiah was in worship and has a vision of God's glory in the temple. He may even have been fasting, although we're not told. What we *do* know is that he encounters the holiness of God, hearing seraphim-angels proclaiming, 'Holy, holy, holy is the LORD Almighty' and his heart is exposed, so much so that he declares 'I am a man of unclean lips.' Then 'one of the seraphim flew to [him] with a live coal in his hands, which he had taken with tongs from the altar'. His mouth is touched and cleansed through the fire of this encounter. Similarly, as we open our hearts to the forge of fasting in worship, we welcome the Lord's perfecting and purifying work in our hearts.

I once spoke with a Christian friend who told me that they used to fast years ago and saw many benefits of it. However, the more they fasted the more they noticed that the hunger made them grumpy. As many of us know, becoming irritable is a very common reaction to feeling hungry, so much so that there's a relatively new word for it in the English language: feeling *hangry*, which is a mixture of being hungry and angry! My friend told me they didn't like this crabby feeling, determining it wasn't a fruit of the Holy Spirit and they had stopped fasting, concluding it wasn't working. But perhaps it *was* working. What if it was doing its convicting role: exposing attitudes and motivations which require transformation?

2. Sanctification
Second, my passions are affected when fasting through intentional *sanctification*.

This is about fasting in order to deliberately invite the Spirit's transformative presence in my heart. I come expectant, knowing that through fasting the Lord reveals unhelpful competitors to my affections which I want knocked off their pedestals, so Christ can take his rightful place. Fasting in this way is about choosing to be holy and desiring heart-change. Basil the Great, greatly respected in Orthodoxy, taught this, saying 'when a fast . . . is introduced into the soul, it kills the sin that lurks deep within'.[21]

I have fasted like this on a number of occasions, especially when I've recognised an unhealthy pattern of selfishness in my life that I want to change. I've done what Origen taught his people to do: to 'fast from every sin',[22] asking the Lord to break its power in my life. I've done this wanting the root of the sin to be exposed and cleansed, identifying with the prayer of David in Psalm 139:23–24 when he prays:

> Search me, God, and know my heart; test me and know my anxious thoughts. See if there is any offensive way in me, and lead me in the way everlasting.

Fasting in this way has been a means of expressing more sincerely that powerful phrase from the Lord's Prayer: 'Forgive us our sins as we forgive those who sin against us.'[23] I believe it has helped me become more prayerful and honest about my frailty and failures, enabling me to come honestly before the Lord.

3. Adoration

Third, my heart is changed when fasting through authentic *adoration*.

This is about fasting for the purpose of worship. It's about turning my heart to the Lord and giving him my love as I become 'a living sacrifice, holy and pleasing to God' which, according to Romans 12:1–2 is 'true . . . worship'. Authentic worship like this always has a knock-on effect on us because, as theologian Tom Wright says, 'we become like what we worship'.[24] That's why I normally spend particular time in worship when fasting. I do this first to give God praise but I know the bi-product is often heart-change.

In preparation I find it good to have helpful worship resources with me when I fast. The most important is the Bible, for it's our worship manual. The Psalms, found in the middle of the Bible, are a particular rich resource for worship. St Athanasius in the fourth century believed so, saying 'Under all circumstances of life, we shall find that these divine songs suit ourselves and meet our own souls' need at every turn.'[25] The Psalms are meant to speak to our hearts, with theologian Paula Gooder saying, 'They take us on a rollercoaster of emotion, from hot to anguish, from praise to fury, from deep calm to utter torment.'[26]

Like many, I sometimes use some set prayers while fasting. Using liturgy in this way can be powerful, especially when certain prayers are repeated again and again to provide focus, to aid memory and show intent. While worship during fasting can take place in silence, I often find spoken prayers and sung worship helpful. Sometimes I will listen to music, especially Christian songs and hymns. I know it's as I worship and 'draw near to God' that 'he will draw near' to me[27] and my heart is changed.

In the Orthodox Church, this adoration is aided by the use of icons in worship, which are sacred images that convey spiritual truth in pictorial form. Icons are meant to turn our hearts to God, which is why they're sometimes described as windows to heaven. Orthodox Christians honour icons but they don't worship them. Those who create icons often consider them to be a form of 'writing' rather than 'painting' because of the teaching they contain, produced after considered study, meditation and prayer. What many outside the Orthodox Church don't realise, is that icon-makers also fast while producing their craft. Indeed they wouldn't consider doing their work without prayerful fasting as the art requires their hearts to be transformed so their imaginations can be liberated and creativity released, resulting in these powerful forms of art. I find this fascinating. Icons help us see the power of fasting *in* worship, *for* worship.

4. Transformation
Fourth, heart-change takes place when fasting through cognitive *transformation*.

This is about God's Spirit transforming not only my desires but my very thoughts. Catholic writer and spiritual director Mary Margaret Funk speaks of this, saying, 'Food is a way of getting to know your thoughts' and that through fasting 'we are "in training" for controlling other thoughts.'[28] Many are not aware that we can change the way we think, but we can. For some, this can become more difficult as we get older, as there's a human tendency to become set in our ways, but for many, and especially for followers of Jesus, that doesn't need to be the case for we know that there's so much to keep learning about life, the world, ourselves and God. We therefore need to be open and attentive to the Spirit. In particular it's good to have Christ in focus, with many in the Orthodox tradition finding the 'Jesus Prayer' helpful, praying on the inhale: 'Lord Jesus Christ, Son of God,' and on the exhale: 'have mercy on me, a sinner.' The aim is prayerfulness, learning to 'pray without ceasing' as Paul says in 1 Thessalonians 5:17 (KJV). Mind-change is a strong biblical theme, with the Scriptures urging Christ-followers to 'be transformed by the renewing of your mind',[29] and that we should think about 'whatever is true, whatever is noble, whatever is right, whatever is pure, whatever is lovely, whatever is admirable – if anything is excellent or praiseworthy'.[30]

We have already noted medical evidence that fasting can help sharpen our thinking. As this takes place alongside a mind focused on Christ and seeking the renewal of the heart, a catalytical reaction can happen in us, as we're changed to think differently, increasingly having the 'mind of Christ'.[31] I know something of this, although I'm aware this doesn't mean I have every answer or get everything right, but it does mean that the wisdom of God, which he loves to give by his Spirit,[32] is imparted. Sometimes I know what to do in a situation where before I was confused. Or I'm clear who to choose for a leadership role. Or I understand what is required to reach a way forward in a particular situation. It can be powerful when a group fasts and then the decision is made together at the end. But don't forget, all this must come from renewed hearts. It's not just becoming smarter, it's becoming holier. Tim Keller was right when he said, 'We must not settle for an informed mind without an enlarged heart.'[33]

5. Action
Fifth, fasting changes my heart through ennobled *action*.

As fasting works on my affections – that is, the desires of my heart – I'm called not only to think differently, but to act differently. I have experienced this on a number of occasions, coming out of a fast knowing I must live differently. At times I've recognised that I must spend more time with one or more members of my family, or give priority to certain people in need or in poverty. Also, I often come out of fasting with a renewed prayer-list of people and situations for which I want to intercede. Righteous action is meant to be aided by the heart-change which comes from prayer and fasting, as American civil rights leader and preacher Martin Luther King taught. He often spoke in the 1960s of this change of heart leading to a change in actions, challenging all ethnic groups to become more compassionate in heart towards others. Citing the teachings of Jesus, he sometimes referred to the rich fool, whose life was a mirror where he saw only his own needs and not those of others. He even spoke of Dives, who 'went to hell, not because he was wealthy, but because he was not tenderhearted enough'.[34]

If we want to become more compassionate, as Jesus advocates in Luke 4, we need to first humble ourselves and pray, making ourselves hungry and fast. Jennifer Miskov understands this, saying, 'The sacrifice of fasting serves the purpose of helping us yield our hearts more fully to Him. If our fasting doesn't lead us to have a more tender heart, respond more swiftly to the leading of the Holy Spirit, move with compassion, love the lost, give to the needy, then we are not doing it right.'[35]

So, these five heart-effects of fasting have many benefits, and I believe they've helped me as I seek to become more conformed to the image of Christ – although there's still much work to do! The aim, in the end, is that fasting will enable us to desire what God desires. To fast in this way is to do what Paul told his young apprentice Timothy to do, when he said, in 1 Timothy 4:7, 'train yourself to be godly'. This, as James K.A. Smith says, is about 'the recalibration of our heart-habits and the recapturing of our imagination, which happens when God's Word becomes the orienting center of our social imaginary, shaping our very perception of things before we even *think* about them'.[36]

Reflection

One of the best ways to encourage and chart this heart-change is to journal as you fast, recording your fasting experience by reflecting on what you're discovering. Journalling is a powerful tool which most people can use. All that's required is a notebook and pen and space to start writing. Journalling is not about diarying what's happening but about reflecting on your response.

Jennifer Miskov encourages people to journal while fasting in this way. Here are some useful questions she considers:

> During a fast, be aware of what comes up for you and take time to journal and process it. Are you easily irritated, feeling out of control, or experiencing some other extreme mood shift? What things are you running to rather than food? What themes are emerging in your heart? What relationships are being brought to the surface, and is He

asking you to respond in a certain way? Is there anyone you need to forgive or be reconciled with? Is there anyone you need to reach out to or become more aligned with?[37]

As someone who both fasts and journals, I have found that the two disciplines sit very well together. While I didn't write specifically about fasting in *The Art of Journalling*,[38] there are many references to fasting in my personal journals and I recommend to people who fast that they should journal while fasting, as much as they can. Here's a typical entry in my journal:

Monday 30th January 2017

So, the twenty-one Days of Prayer and Fasting are finished. I've found it hard but rewarding. Lots of people have been touched. People have put their faith in Christ . . . Some healings. Some genuine encounters with the Lord . . .

It's been good, but next time I must clear my diary more. I've been too busy so I personally haven't benefited as much as I could. But I have prayed with lots of people. So, help me Lord to plan better next time.

Emotion

As we become more reflective and self-aware through fasting, so we get to know ourselves better, and also become more attentive to the work of the Spirit of God in our lives and communities. In doing this, it's important to take note of the emotions that we feel. That of course is true of life in general, for we want to be emotionally intelligent people (what's often called people with 'EQ'), who read wisely the emotions of people around us. But this emotional intelligence can also relate to ourselves, as we consider our own emotional responses. I've found this in recent years, discovering fasting to be a great context for emotional learning.

For example, I've found it helpful to recognise, name and turn to prayer the emotions I experience from *the feeling of hunger*. Unwelcome emotions that I've noticed have included irritability, frustration, stress and lethargy. I know some feel anxiety, anger and sorrow. Even seasoned fasters can sometimes feel these especially when hunger first kicks in when fasting. I pray about these, and hand them over to the Lord. I might seek understanding, asking if there's a particular reason why they're there, and I invite the Lord to perfect them and use them to renew me. Helpful emotions might include gratitude, wonder, contentment and optimism, and I similarly offer them in prayer, asking that my heart would be set on fire with love for God.

However, when fasting I've also learned to attend to the emotions I feel for *the things I'm praying about*. Sometimes these emotions seem to be enhanced when I fast, which can be really helpful. So, when I'm fasting and praying for a particular matter and feel compassion rise for a person or situation, I take note of this and it helps me to pray with compassion. When I feel expectant, or excited, or joyful, or concerned, or frustrated, or angry, or whatever emotion comes, I've been learning to take these emotions seriously and turn them to prayer, finding they enhance the body-prayer that is already taking place as I make my whole being hungry through fasting. As I do this, it feels like the Spirit of God is helping me to pray, in my weakness and vulnerability. The apostle Paul speaks in similar terms to this when he writes of prayer in Romans 8, describing emotional 'groaning as in the pains of childbirth' and that 'the Spirit helps us in our weakness' for although 'we do not know what we ought to pray for . . . the Spirit himself intercedes for us' (v.26). While there is no specific mention of fasting in Romans 8, Paul does talk about 'bodies', prayer, 'hearts' and 'weakness', which as we've been discovering are all big fasting themes.

For these reasons and more, I encourage those fasting to pay attention to their emotions as they fast. While we're not to be governed by our feelings but by God's unchanging Word, we must still take seriously our emotions, because they can help us understand not only how *we* feel about situations, and also how the *Holy Spirit* feels about them. As we cooperate with the Holy Spirit, so we learn to become more emotionally intelligent with regard to God – what some call *spiritually intelligent*, having 'SQ' – as we seek to understand how *God* feels. We want our heart to feel God's heart so, like David, we become someone 'after [God's] own heart'.[39]

Little research has been done on the place of emotions in fasting. I would be fascinated to see the results and especially if more emotionally demonstrative cultures engage in prayerful fasting more naturally in this way. Samuel Chadwick, a pioneering Methodist prayer leader of the early twentieth century and mentor to my grandfather seems to suggest so, saying, 'Prayers are measured neither by time nor by number but by intensity.'[40] Chadwick believed in passionate, emotive praying, as did his student Leonard Ravenhill, who preached and taught about prayer being central to revival. Ravenhill exclaimed: 'The two prerequisites of successful Christian living are vision and passion, both of which are born in and maintained by prayer.'[41] Fervent, heartfelt, emotive prayer, aided by fasting is likely to be a most potent spiritual cocktail.

Protection

Given our heart if so central to our wellbeing, it's important that we look after it. That's why the Bible urges God's people to 'guard your heart, for it is the wellspring of life'.[42] The state of our heart will determine whether what we share with the world is refreshing and renewing, or polluting and profane. It's paramount, then, that we protect our hearts, ensuring they're healthy and not sick; tender and not hard; kind and not cruel. How do we do this? As we've seen, followers of Jesus do this by welcoming the Spirit's presence in our hearts, so we become more like Jesus. Ephesians 6 tells us to take up the 'shield of faith' which guards our heart against 'all the flaming arrows of the evil one' (v.16), which should lead us to pray (vv.18–20). Prayer protects the heart, as we ask God to 'lead us not into temptation, but deliver us from the evil one'[43] and, as we've been discovering, it's especially aided by the discipline of fasting.

Basil the Great understood this. He knew that prayerful fasting helps protect the heart, especially against forces of darkness that want to hinder good things flowing from us to others. He even taught that 'the demons dare not hurl insults at the one who fasts'[44] which doesn't mean that Satan won't confront those who fast, for he certainly challenged Jesus while he was fasting and he might do the same for us, but it does mean that there's a protective nature to prayer with fasting. Jesus modelled this in his temptations, as well as in his ministry, and ultimately in his resurrection, where the forces of darkness failed to triumph. This is all the more reason to guard our hearts by prayer and fasting.

Having said all this, it's sobering to recognise that fasting by itself doesn't automatically guard our hearts or bring heart-change, as Jesus makes clear in Luke 18:9–14, telling a story of a pious religious leader and a corrupt tax collector. Both go to the Jerusalem temple to pray. The tax collector is truly sorry and remorseful for his selfishness. The religious leader sees the tax collector and pridefully thanks God that he is not a sinner like him, and reminds God that he tithes his money and fasts regularly. Jesus concludes that it's not the fasting religious leader who 'went home justified before God' but the tax collector. Why? Because the religious leader displays no mercy, showing that his fasting has not changed his heart.

Character

So, how does fasting change our hearts? The answer, as we've been seeing, is to fast prayerfully, allowing fasting to do its exposing work and become a holiness tool, forming righteous character in us and making us more into the likeness of Christ. We all need this, which is why eighteenth-century Baptist pastor Andrew Fuller said, 'Fasting is supposed to be the ordinary practice of the godly.'[45] This heart-formation takes place within the family of God's church, as we support each other and grow in holiness together, becoming more Christ-like, being shaped into the 'Blessed' ones named in the Beatitudes (in Matthew 5:3–11) in Jesus' Sermon on the Mount. If we want to reflect this loving heart of Jesus, we must embrace these God-like dispositions of the heart, which especially develop through the discipline of fasting.

So having discovered (in chapter one) that fasting is about hunger as we restrict intake into our *mouths*, and then (in chapter two) that fasting is about holiness as God's Spirit is welcomed to change our *hearts*, so the focus of our next chapter is on *hands,* as we consider all sorts of practical questions about *The Art of Fasting*.

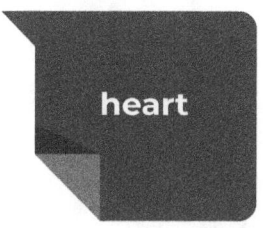

- fasting opens our hearts and exposes our desires
- fasting reveals what controls us
- fasting softens, matures and protects our hearts
- fasting heightens our emotions
- fasting gives us righteous loving hearts like Jesus

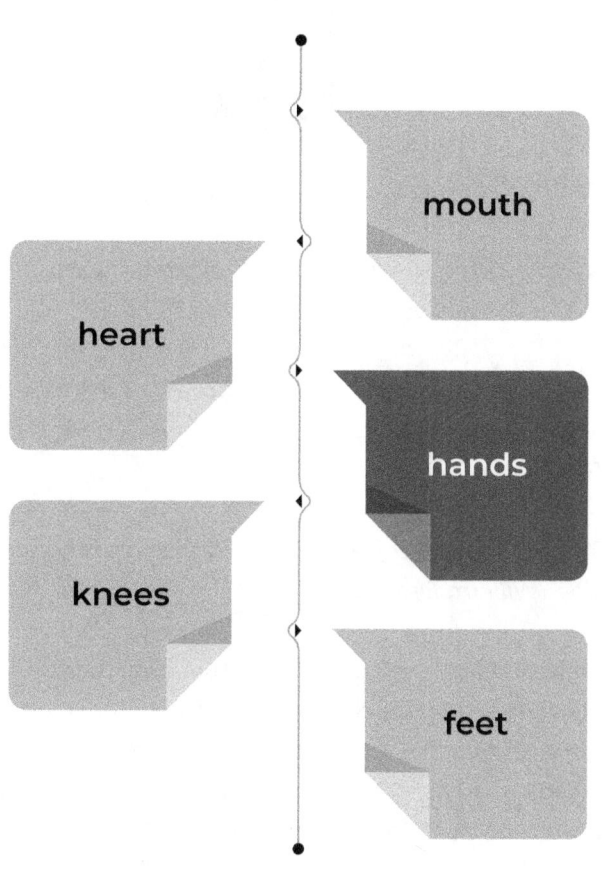

Chapter 3

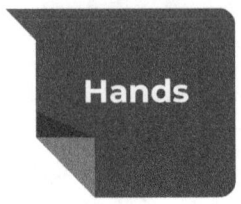

- *'Strengthen the weak hands' (Isaiah 35:3).*

- *'Whatever your hand finds to do, do it with all your might' (Ecclesiastes 9:10).*

- *'We know that the way to move information from your head to your heart is through your hands' (Brené Brown).*[1]

- *'Artists, after all, think with their hands and their fingertips' (William Dryness).*[2]

Rock bands like their pre-stage rituals. The band U2 normally gather in a circle and read from *The Message* – Eugene Peterson's modern translation of the Bible. 'It has been a great strength to me', says lead singer Bono, describing how Peterson's work 'brought the text back to the tone in which the books were written.'[3] Peterson's contemporary language paraphrase completed in 2002 has helped a generation of new readers to hear the Scriptures with fresh imagination. Peterson also wrote other books,

Hands

all with thoughtful titles, many of which have profoundly shaped their readers, including me. One, rather than being a book *translating* the Bible is a book *about* the Bible, encouraging readers how to read it well; it has the aptly named title: *Eat This Book*.

Written when in his seventies, *Eat This Book* picks up a phrase that appears particularly in the colourful and challenging Bible books of Ezekiel[4] and Revelation,[5] expressing Peterson's passionate desire for God's message to become embodied and lived in ordinary people. Peterson expressed it in the Preface like this: 'for over fifty years now I have been vocationally involved in getting the Christian Scriptures into the minds and hearts, arms and legs, ears and mouths of men and women. And I haven't found it easy.'[6] The reason, he says, is that while many read the Bible to gain understanding, 'what is neglected is reading the Scriptures formatively, reading in order to live'. That's why *Eat This Book* is very practical, offering not only wise teaching but helpful advice on ways to get the Bible *into* us, so it can flow *out of* us into the world. From his vast experience Peterson knew that the way from the head and the heart is through the hands.

This chapter is all about our hands. It's about how we use our hands in *The Art of Fasting*, as we choose to eat and not eat. To feast and fast. It's about the *doing* of fasting, describing in very practical ways *how* we can fast, especially as we feast on Christ and his Word. It's a very hands-on chapter, getting into some of the nitty-gritty aspects of fasting and answering some of the main questions that I'm often asked about fasting.

Anna

One person who fasted in the Bible is an elderly woman named Anna. We discover Anna in Luke 2, which describes her meeting with Joseph and Mary, the parents of Jesus:

> There was also a prophet, Anna, the daughter of Penuel, of the tribe of Asher. She was very old; she had lived with her husband seven years after her marriage, and then was a widow until she was eighty-four. She never left the temple but worshipped night and day, fasting and praying. Coming up to them at that very moment, she gave thanks to God and spoke about the child to all who were looking forward to the redemption of Jerusalem.
>
> *Luke 2:36–38*

Anna fasted, knowing that 'fasting and praying' go together. Her story helps us as we consider in this chapter the practicalities of fasting, recognising – as we're seeing – that while Christian fasting involves denying our body food, it's also meant to be a prayerful discipline, particularly used in the context of worship, and is about turning our hearts to God. It's noteworthy that Anna not only fasted in the day, but often at night, so it wasn't just an occasional discipline which she exercised at convenient times, but instead was a deliberate, embodied act that she regularly practised, seeing all times of day or night as available for fasting. It also seems that this habit stirred and encouraged her prophetic gift, for when the infant Jesus was in the temple with his parents, the fasting Anna was drawn to him, intuitively knowing he was special, and then telling others what she had encountered. It seems that fasting empowered Anna in her life and calling.

Anglicanism

Anna's story raises lots of questions, like: Why did she fast? How might she have fasted? And how can and should *we* practise this discipline? For the last 500 years the Anglican Church has asked good questions like that about many aspects of faith, including the subject of fasting, and it offers us some welcome resources for practicing this discipline wisely and well.

In this chapter, following the example of Anna, and mining the vein of resources partly in Anglicanism but also beyond, we'll consider twelve very practical questions about fasting, namely:

1. For how long should we limit our food intake? And how often?

2. What about fluids?
3. Are there different types of fast?
4. What about those who can't fast from food?
5. How do we prepare well to fast?
6. What should we be doing when we're fasting?
7. How should we end a fast?
8. What difficulties can arise when we fast?
9. How can we fast together?
10. Is it possible to fast badly?
11. Is fasting just for followers of Jesus?
12. If I've never fasted, where do I begin?

Length

1: For how long should we limit our food intake? And how often?

There's no prescribed length of fasting in the Bible. That means that fasting for one meal is a valid form of fasting. In the Jewish tradition people would often fast from sunset to sunset, with Jewish rabbis fasting on Mondays and Thursdays. In *The Didache*, one of the earliest Christian documents, dated around the end of the first century, Christians are encouraged to fast on Wednesdays and Fridays, and the Orthodox Church today continues to teach this, as we've seen. For Muslims, fasting is one of their five Pillars of Faith and in Ramadan they don't eat food or water during daylight hours.

Hands

Down the centuries many have fasted as part of their regular rhythm of life, including it as part of their weekly pattern of devotion. I have often done this, so when I was vicar of St Chad's Church in Woodseats in Sheffield, I would fast on Thursdays as part of a weekly Prayer Day we introduced, inviting the church to pray for various matters and to come to one of four prayer gatherings held across the day.[7] Others fast as one-offs, doing so when sensing a need or the prompting of the Holy Spirit to do so. As I write this book in the early mornings during the season of Lent, I'm fasting breakfast, which means not eating from bedtime one day until lunch the next. I break this fast on my weekly rest day.

Sometimes it's right to fast for longer than a day. I have fasted for a number of days for a variety of reasons, although I have not (yet) undergone a long fast. John Sentamu, when he was Anglican Archbishop of York, fasted for a week in the summer of 2005, pitching a tent in a side-chapel of York Minster, as he prayed for peace in the Middle East. The Bible describes some people fasting for up to forty days which a few still practise occasionally today, although such a long fast must be undertaken with great care and with good medical advice. While not wanting to exclude this possibility, we should be aware that the biblical notion of 'forty days' can be a way of describing *a long time* rather than a specific number.

Many church traditions fast corporately at certain times of the year, from holy days to liturgical seasons and especially in Lent, although this was often emphasised much more strongly in the past than it is today, with the Church of England's contemporary prayer book, called *Common Worship*, introduced in 2000 no longer speaking of 'Days of Fasting' but instead of 'Days of Discipline and Self Denial'. Nicholas Sagovsky, who was canon theologian at Westminster Abbey, reflects on this change by saying that 'Fasting has largely become a matter of personal choice.'[8]

It seems, then, that there's much liberty when it comes to the length of fasting. We need to hear this, because like all disciplines, we often want to get into the detail and if we're not careful we can become rather fixated by goals and targets and how well we're doing. While this might be understandable, especially when starting out, we need to get beyond that and learn to enjoy the discipline and relax into it. While sometimes *the exact length* of the fast may seem important, what's more significant is what happens *while* we fast.

When considering how often we should fast, I see some similarities with financial giving. In the same way that giving money is best practised both regularly and occasionally, so I encourage church leaders to do the same with fasting, setting a good example by fasting in both a disciplined and spontaneous way.

Drink

2: What about fluids?

The normal means of Christian fasting includes drinking fluids, particularly water. Shatin Church in Hong Kong, for example, is a contemporary Anglican church that has regular fasting days and says: 'We are encouraging people to fast that day – to just drink water the whole day, until our fellowship meal after the meeting.'[9] While some occasionally fast from both food *and water*, avoiding water should not be undertaken regularly or for more than twenty-four hours, as our bodies need regular liquid to survive and thrive.

As well as water some drink other fluids, such as juice or even supplements. A few might include soup, which can be helpful in a long fast, but given that soups can just be liquidised meals with high calorie content, we mustn't fool ourselves into thinking that 'drinking' soup is a normative and biblical means of fasting. It's not.

Alcohol is not normally consumed during a fast, as the brain-altering and intoxicating effects of alcohol increase on an empty stomach. Some continue to drink tea and coffee, especially on short fasts. There are no rules about this. If you drink coffee regularly like I do, be aware that if you stop for a day or more you are likely to get headaches, sometimes severely, until your body has detoxed. I know this experience and it is sometimes unpleasant but worth pushing through.

Types
3: Are there different types of fast?

The typical fast, as we've seen, involves voluntarily not eating food, but there are other kinds of fasts too, with four being particularly common.

First, there is *The Ascetic Fast*. This is continuing to eat but restricting intake of food. It often involves avoiding sugar and sweet foods, with many doing this today when giving up chocolate for Lent. The Anglican Church has often encouraged this, and it's reflected in the practice of making pancakes on Shrove Tuesday, the day before Lent, in order to use up all the sweet things in the house before the season of Lent. Some restrict their diet by engaging in what's sometimes called 'The Daniel Fast'. Following the example of Daniel in Daniel 10, this is a restricted diet of fruit and vegetables. I have used this fast a few times during Lent, missing lunch with the evening meal being only of fruit and vegetables. Not only can it have health benefits, especially for a season, but some of the fasting benefits we saw in chapter one can be experienced by fasting in this way. Also be aware it can produce much gastric wind, especially if your stomach is not used to such a diet!

Second, there is *The Simplicity Fast*, which instead of abstaining from food involves cutting out certain activities that we'd normally practise. For example, we might decide not to use technology for a day, avoiding the television and radio. For many this will involve turning off social media feeds and even locking your phone away to minimise distractions. These are fasting-like, and can have many benefits, but should not be used as an alternative to never fasting food (unless we can't for health reasons), for biblical fasting is about making our bodies hungry, so we hunger for God.

Third, there is *The Alcohol Fast*. This involves abstaining from alcohol or any other stimulant, for a day, or perhaps a week, or season. People who practise this often find it has a detoxifying effect on the body, with their mind becoming clearer. Basil the Great agreed, saying, 'if you wish to make your mind strong, subdue your flesh through fasting'.[10]

Fourth, there is the *Sex Fast*. This is when a married couple choose not to make love for a period of time. Sam and I practised this once during the forty-six days of Lent in the early years of our marriage, and it was both a fascinating and frustrating time, when we learned a lot about ourselves and each other, each writing a personal journal of our reflections and prayers which we shared with each other. We used the time to particularly pray about a couple of matters. The New Testament encourages married couples to practice a sex fast from time to time, and to use the time for prayer, also encouraging them to end it by enjoying healthy regular sex afterwards.[11]

These last two fasts – *The Alcohol Fast* and *The Sex Fast* – are, according to Scripture, fasts that all should practise from time to time, and for some they are permanent fasts. *The Alcohol Fast* in the Old Testament was practised by all priests when they were on duty in the temple, no doubt to ensure their minds were sharp and not distracted from the task of serving the Lord and his people. The New Testament does not preclude drinking alcohol, but does say we should not get drunk or let what we take into our bodies cause others 'to fall'.[12] Like anything we do, we should also be able to say 'no' to it, to show that it doesn't master us, which no doubt means there should be times for all Christ-followers when they don't drink alcohol. In addition, some people are called to avoid alcohol permanently. This was the case for the Nazirites in the Old Testament,[13] and for John the Baptist in the New,[14] and for some the Holy Spirit permanently calls them to this, and I am one of those.[15] *The Sex Fast*, as we've seen, is something married people are called to practise occasionally, especially when praying for a particular matter, and it should be a permanent fast for all except those who are married. In these days of few sexual boundaries with consenting adults experimenting in all sorts of sexual practices, the Scriptures invite followers of Jesus to live differently and restrict sex to the committed, exclusive and diverse relationship of a husband-wife marriage.[16]

Health
4: What about those who can't fast from food?

Some people can't fast for health reasons. This is either due to a medical condition causing their body to require regular food, or because they have an eating disorder that would be exacerbated by fasting. There is no shame in this. If that's you, while you will not be able to receive all the benefits of fasting from food, you should still be able to practise some of the other types of fasting mentioned in Q3, especially *The Simplicity Fast* which includes things like not connecting with social media or TV. For those who can't fast from food, embrace these fasts with prayer and passion, intent and joy!

Given that fasting involves a healthy identification with people in poverty, those who cannot fast from food can find other ways to do this, perhaps living on a lower income level for a while and giving the money away to assist those in poorer nations. Many Anglican churches and their clergy have encouraged such practices, particularly in recent years, as the reality of world hunger has become more apparent and widely seen on our television screens.

Fasting is normally for healthy adults and should not be imposed on babies or young children or the elderly or infirm. However, some children or pensioners may wish to join in limited fasting, and with careful monitoring this should be encouraged. Those with diabetes should not fast, and particularly those with dietary issues and intestinal complications. People menstruating or with post-natal bleeding are often advised to take care, as are those on particular medication. Studies suggest there's no particular reason why pregnant women should not fast for a short time, unless they have particular medical issues.

If you're unsure about any particular condition, always consult a qualified medical practitioner for advice.

Before
5: How do we prepare well to fast?

Before you fast it's good to prepare carefully. Here are three things you can do.

First, *prepare your time*. Look at your diary and be aware of what you'll be doing as you fast. Is your diary clear to do whatever you want? Or is it a normal working day? Or is it something in-between? If you can clear some focused time, most of us can, you will find this beneficial. For example, if you normally take forty minutes to eat lunch at work, and you're going to fast instead, highlight that lunchtime slot for a particularly focused prayer time. That doesn't mean that the rest of the time is unimportant – in fact, far from it, for if you are attentive to your body, you will sense the growing hunger as the day goes on. You can plan to use this background sense of hunger as an offering to God even if your mind is focused on whatever task is before you.

Second, *prepare your body*. If your fast is going to be short, there will be less need for this. If it is to be more than a day, some cut back on sugar ahead of time, while also increasing carbohydrates (like potatoes) and protein (like meat or beans). If you know you're likely to get headaches from caffeine withdrawal, you could begin to limit your caffeine intake slowly over a few days, to lessen the impact. Drinking water is always a good thing to do, whether fasting or not, and it can be a good way too to prepare your body for a fast.

Third, *prepare your heart*. Recognise that Christian fasting is not just a *physical* matter, so take stock of the state of your heart. Ask yourself why you are going to fast, recognising not only the things you would like to offer to God during the fast, but your motives too. Take note of your hopes for your fast, and if you can, write them down in your journal. And most importantly, pray. Ask the Spirit of God, who is leading you into this fast, to help you prepare well. In particular consider if there's a section of the Bible on which you might focus. Jesus probably did this when he fasted in the wilderness, as all his responses to the devil's testing came from the book of Deuteronomy, which is likely to be the text he was reflecting on while fasting.[17] If you plan to read a particular book, or draw or paint or make something creative while you fast, you will need to gather resources. It's all part of being ready.

During
6: What should we be doing when we're fasting?

First consider if there are things that it would be best *not* to do. For example, experts tell us that we need to take care doing vigorous exercise while fasting as we may well burn fat more quickly, so if you regularly work out, you might want to pause while fasting. Then also think about what you *will* do, and the main thing I recommend is to give time for prayerful reflection. Reflection, as I say in *The Art of Journalling*, is about deep thinking,[18] and fasting is a great door-opener for this, enabling us to process well, particularly as we pray and read the Bible.

Prayer is key to reflection, so seek a prayerful disposition while fasting. The Lord's Prayer is the central prayer of the church,[19] and is useful in any context, especially when fasting, so pray it. This can be done in its entirety (in one go), perhaps praying it at the beginning and end of a fast or even hourly, or it can be prayed in chunks, pausing for silence of extemporary prayer, speaking to God from the heart. I often use the Lord's Prayer, or parts of it, when fasting. Based on the words of Jesus in Matthew 6:9–13, I begin with worship, telling the Lord how much I appreciate him and giving him my grateful thanks ('Our Father in heaven, hallowed be your name'). Often I will want to pray prayers of intercession, calling out to God to bring his transformative kingdom ('Your kingdom come') and his godly will to bear in our world, and in the lives of the people for whom I am praying ('your will be done, on earth as it is in heaven'). I can also pray prayers of supplication for myself and others, asking our good Father for provision ('Give us this day our daily bread'), forgiveness ('Forgive us our sins, as we forgive those who sin against us'), and protection ('Lead us not into temptation, but deliver us from evil'), and ending in praise ('For the kingdom, the power, and the glory are yours now and for ever. Amen').[20] Prayer and fasting are meant to go together, so don't hold back from prayer. Speak to the Lord and ask him for all that is needed and keep practising because, as Anglican priest and evangelist David Watson recognised, 'there is nothing more difficult in the Christian life, because there is nothing more powerful or spiritual than prayer'.[21] That's why I use a variety of prayer tools to help me, including speaking in tongues.[22] Many have found fasting to be a great context to use tongues, offering your heartfelt and thankful praise and prayers to God. If you don't exercise that gift, fasting is a good opportunity to ask. I know some who have received it while fasting.

Reading the Bible is also very important when it comes to reflecting well, as reading Scripture feeds not just our minds, but our souls. That's why Jill Duff, Anglican bishop of Lancaster, says, 'I read the Bible every day. I try to get to know parts off by heart. It feeds me . . . '[23] Indeed, Bible-reading helps us feast while we fast, for instead of feasting on food, we feast on Christ who is the *Living Word*, by reading the Bible which is his *written Word*. Jesus recognised this while he fasted, saying, 'Man shall not live on bread alone, but on every word that comes from the mouth of God.'[24] By this he's referring to the Scriptures which, as we saw at the start of this chapter when considering Eugene Peterson's writing, we're urged to eat and digest. Seasoned faster Heidi Baker has found this, saying: 'I've heard other people say that when they are fasting, they have nightly dreams and visions. For me, I am just hungry a lot of the time. But I spend a lot of time reading the Word of God.'[25] Like many, she finds feasting on God's Word during fasting to be supremely nourishing.

Don't forget too that fasting is part of the slow work of discipleship. Fasting can't and shouldn't be rushed. We need to let its unhurried work effect our bodies and minds and hearts. So, if we can slow ourselves down, especially when on a longer fast, that will enable us to consciously share in this powerful, steady, unrushed work of the Holy Spirit, in a relaxed and joyful manner. This can be hard if slowing down has the initial effect of cluttering our minds (which it sometimes does – see question 8 below), but once we're past that we find that fasting helps us to focus, to pray, and to feast on the bread of life, who is Jesus Christ.

After
7: How should we end a fast?

It's good to think through the transition out of fasting, especially if you've been fasting for more than twenty-four hours. You will be hungry, but it's good not to eat a large meal immediately, as that can put a strain on your digestive system, so don't wolf down your food, but take it slowly, chewing well. Those things might be obvious but are worth remembering! Some nutritionists recommend soups and not having anything sugary or carbohydrate-rich too quickly. It can be a good thing to end a shared fast with a shared meal as we'll consider in question 9. Also, don't forget to enjoy eating after a fast! That was not only allowed but commended by some early church fathers, who said that 'fasting enhances the enjoyment of food when it is partaken'.[26]

Given that fasting should change our hearts, it's good to think and pray about what you'll be going into straight after the fast. If it's going to be a difficult meeting or heavy work schedule, or even a celebratory family occasion, the fast is a good opportunity to prepare yourself and ensure your attitude is good and that you're attentive and ready to be fully present and contribute well. Some will choose to end a fast by taking bread and wine in a service of Holy Communion with others. This often occurs at the end of Anglican contemplative retreats and can be a wonderful way to enter again into the regular rhythms of eating and living, as the eucharistic elements are savoured and enjoyed, and we give thanks for all that Christ is and has done for us.

Difficulties

8: What difficulties can arise when we fast?

Fasting brings lots of benefits, but it's not all plain-sailing. In fact, breaking the routine of eating can be a shock to your body, your mind and your heart, especially if you've not fasted for a while. You may not be used to that empty feeling in the stomach, so you might want to start with just one meal to begin. Some people say they can't fast because when they try, they feel ill. As we've seen, that can be true for a few people, but most can, but to do so we may need first to disassociate feeling hungry from feeling ill. Let me explain. When we're unwell our bodies often don't want to eat, and we get that empty feeling in our stomach. If being ill is the only time we have that empty-stomach feeling, it's easy to see how we might think feeling hungry is the same as feeling ill, but it's not. We need to learn to distinguish between the two.

You might find you feel light-headed, especially after about half a day, or you start to get headaches as your body begins to detox from various products that are no longer feeding it, especially caffeine. Once when I fasted, the headaches became a migraine and I felt genuinely ill and terribly nauseous. I had to go home, have some bread and water to settle my stomach and put myself to bed and sleep off the pain. That kind of thing has been rare for me, but it can happen and it's a good reminder that sometimes it's right to break a fast. There's no need for embarrassment if that's necessary.

When fasting you may feel tired and want to sleep at certain points; depending on your plans and schedule that might be no bad thing, especially as you can be prayerful as you drop off, being attentive to any dreams, as well as your waking thoughts.[27] Some feel irritable and on edge when fasting, and it is good to record that, and ask God to be at work in our hearts.

Often when we fast and make space to slow down and pray, we find our minds initially become filled with so many thoughts that it's hard to focus. There are a variety of ways to handle that. What I often do is have a notebook near me, and I simply write them all down. They may well be things I need to do later, like an email to send, or something mundane that needs adding to the shopping list. There might be other things, like recalling a person in need, or a situation in the world. While those things may feel like distractions that need to be noted on paper for afterwards, I've learned that sometimes one or more of those can be things that the Spirit of God is bringing to mind for me to pray about while fasting. That's why you need to be prayerful as you scribble, so you can discern the difference between the mind decluttering and the Spirit directing. Once the thoughts start to go onto paper, I find my mind begins to clear and settle.

Sometimes when we fast, our minds can wander onto unhelpful things as our hearts and desires are revealed. It is possible, like Jesus in the wilderness, that we are being tempted, especially if we feel we are being enticed into thinking in ways that are dark or destructive. When that happens, I've learned to be honest about those things, finding a way to express them, either by journalling or perhaps drawing a picture or writing down a single word. This can feel uncomfortable and exposing and might need processing with a wise friend or spiritual director, either at the time or perhaps later. Learning from Jesus, it's likely that the Spirit of God has Scripture ready to speak into these areas, so be attentive to his voice and ask him to cleanse our hearts. Like Jesus when he was tested, the Spirit wants us to come out stronger, not weaker, and so if you feel you're being tempted when fasting, don't feel ashamed but instead see it as a wonderful opportunity for maturity and growth, so you can emerge better equipped for the coming season. As we seek to bring glory to God, are led by the Spirit and feast on Christ, we have nothing to fear.

Some are disappointed at the end of fasting, especially if they hope the fasting experience will be dramatic, or intense, or highly stimulating, and it's not. While dramatic encounters with God can happen when fasting, that has only occasionally been the case for me. More normally, the experience of fasting isn't deeply moving at the time; instead, the personal benefits to me or my prayers come slowly and are often hard to see at first, so I've learned to take the long view. Sometimes after fasting I hear of prayers answered and breakthroughs occurring, and that of course is a great encouragement. Journalling helps me see this, especially if I record in my journal not only prayers but testimonies. Occasionally I re-read my journal and see a link between prayer, fasting and answered prayer. I've seen enough of these to agree with Basil the Great, who said, 'Fasting sends prayer up to heaven, as if it were its wings for the upward journey.'[28] Of course, none of that can be scientifically proved, as like all prayer, the changes seen after prayer might have happened in any event. That's why there's a glorious mystery to fasting.

Finally, it's worth recognising that we're in a spiritual battle and that Satan certainly doesn't want us to pray or fast. So, pray and fast. But be aware that there will be unseen forces in the background seeking to discourage you. There is nothing to worry about here, but we must be wise to the struggles and, if possible, fast with others, and/or have a trusted praying friend supporting us in prayer, while we fast.

Communal
9: How can we fast together?

While some fast on their own, it's good to fast communally. If you live with others, either in a family or shared household of sorts, people will probably know you're fasting. If they ask, of course tell them, just don't brag about it.[29] If you can fast together, even better. This is often aided by having a shared issue to fast about, like a friend who's ill, or a particular need in your life, or household, or community. Throughout church history, many churches have invited their members to fast together for something in particular. Today this might also be done in prayer triplets, or with your small group. It could be that your whole church is invited to fast by the leadership. I've done that in the churches I've led on quite a number of occasions, agreeing first with the other leaders a date, and often a reason, when we will fast together. We've done that, for example, for twenty-one days at the start of the year in January, or during Lent, or in the run-up to a gift day, or at a time of vision-casting that's often linked to a period of Renewal of Financial Giving. When we've done this, we've usually posted on social media and put out a leaflet explaining how people can join in, and inviting everyone, if they can, to fast in some way, so it's a shared and communal activity.

When we fasted at St Michael le Belfrey Church in York in Lent 2023, just a couple of months before I left, we invited people to pray and fast each Thursday, missing lunch if they could in order to pray, and then we met together in church in the early evening for a corporate prayer meeting, which ended with a shared meal together. The prayer meeting was at 6.30 p.m. (rather than our usual 7.30 p.m.), as people didn't need time to eat before coming out, and the meal was served around 8 p.m. We did this aware that many African churches use this simple model of fasting followed by feasting, and it seemed to work well for us in the UK too.

Fasting can also be a corporate activity that we share in beyond our local church, either with other churches in our locality, or with a wider group of people in our town, or city. Eighteenth-century New England preacher Jonathan Edwards found this, saying, 'It seems to me it would be becoming the circumstances of the present day, if ministers in a neighborhood would often meet together and spend days in fasting and fervent prayer among themselves, earnestly seeking for those extraordinary supplies of divine grace from heaven, that we need at this day.'[30] Corporate fasting like this can also extend beyond a city to a region or whole nation. Indeed, occasional national fasts have not been uncommon in British history, and have often been linked to prayer. We saw an example in the story at the start of chapter two, when in 1756 the people of England prayed and fasted successfully for peace.

Unhelpful

10: Is it possible to fast badly?

Yes. Fasting is a good thing to do, but not if our actions are unkind and unjust; if they are, then our fasting is ineffective and worthless. American preacher Randy Clark agrees, saying that in the Bible 'Fasting in the wrong spirit or without humility, without seeking righteousness and justice, is seen in a negative light.'[31] That's why we always need to check our hearts to ensure they're not cold or corrupt and that our actions align. When they do, and we're seeking to serve and not be served, then fasting can be very catalytical, releasing God's power. But if we think we can fast while not caring for people in poverty, or failing to treat our family well, or living selfishly, then we're in for a shock, for *that* kind of fasting is unhelpful and ineffective. It's another reminder that prayer and action always go together.

Inclusive
11: Is fasting just for followers of Jesus?

No. Fasting is a practice that can be exercised by *anyone*. Those with no religious affiliation can still enjoy all sorts of advantages of fasting, but given that the benefits are broad, affecting not just the body and mind but also the heart and soul, it's not surprising that most religions encourage it in some form. However, as we've been seeing, it can easily become a legalistic practice, and so *how* we practise and the attitude with which we fast is crucial. For Muslims, for example, it's a practice that is commanded at certain times, and if missed, you are supposed to pay a Fidya in the form of financial penance. Followers of Jesus approach fasting differently, for fasting is not something they *have* to do. Instead, fasting is commended, not commanded. We're not told we *must*, but it's assumed we *will*. We had a Muslim teenager live with us for a few years who sometimes ate what we were eating and at other times ate halal food. If we were about to enter a period of fasting, we would let him know and sometimes he would ask why, and we explained that there were certain things we wanted to pray about and that fasting helped. When he realised that this was a choice and that we didn't *have* to, he found this very strange. He couldn't understand why anyone would *want* to fast!

Begin

12: If I've never fasted, where do I begin?

It's good to be informed about fasting, and reading a book like this is a good start! But of course, you get to the point when you need to start. Anglican Thomas Becon, writing in 1551, recognised this, saying that having thought and talked much about fasting, now 'let us so much the more gladly exercise the godly manner of fasting'.[32] In short, don't just talk about it, do it! So, make a plan, and look at your upcoming schedule, chose a day in the coming week or two, and write it in your diary, and then start.

I usually advise people to begin by missing one meal, perhaps lunch. Prepare for it for a few days, as advised above. Most importantly, give yourself some space so that the time you would have spent eating lunch is now dedicated to prayer and worship and reading Scripture. Feast on Christ. As you pray, reflect and perhaps write in your journal. As you feel more hungry, especially later in the afternoon while you wait to break your fast with your evening meal, let your body-hunger become part of your prayer, and tell the Lord that you hunger for him, for his kingdom to come and his will to be done in your life and, if there is a situation you are bringing before him, in that context. Recognise that the feeling of hunger is a pang many people in poverty live with every day, as they do not have sufficient food. When you finally eat, give thanks for the food, from a grateful heart.

Afterwards, you might choose to give to charity the money you would have spent on lunch. Also consider talking with a trusted friend about the experience. Begin to learn *The Art of Fasting*. Practised well and regularly, over time, it will help you become a more prayerful person.

Jerry

All this was expressed helpfully to me in an email I received a few years ago from Jerry, a woman at the church I led, who shared with me how she got started with fasting.

February 2019

Hi Matthew,

I've been taking part in the challenge of fasting one meal a week, for three weeks now.

Firstly, just the fact I've been able to fast is an answer to prayer in itself. I have a history of being very controlling/legalistic about my weight and food intake, even having experienced disordered eating in the past. I've been talking to the Lord about it for some time, but progress has been slow...

I've never taken part in previous seasons of fasting at church. So the fact I've been taking part this year is a turn-up for the books.

Secondly, the Lord has generously provided exactly what I need during these fasts. Gosh, it can be hard – but he's given me lots of little encouragements in the form of a kind word from someone who didn't even know I was fasting, a distraction, a verse of Scripture.

Thirdly, the fasting is doing 'what it says on the tin' in terms of seeing God's hand move in a range of situations I'm praying for at present. X is growing, Y was packed to the rafters tonight, we've had an offer on our house, and tons of little arrow prayers for myself and for others have been answered, too. But interestingly, I've found that the issues where I've seen the most change have been the two issues which had stopped me from fasting before – legalism with weight, and being a grumpy mum! I think it's in both these areas that the Lord is ministering to me most.

I couldn't agree more with your analysis that: 'We have such a good Father. A kind, caring, strong, forgiving Father. From him, all good things flow.' Amen!

Thank you for getting a conversation going around the much-overlooked discipline of fasting. And for being an example of someone who fasts – and survives!

Blessings,

Jerry

Jerry's story is powerful and persuasive. It encourages us not just to fast for its physical benefits (chapter one), and to fast to have our hearts changed (chapter two), and to fast with understanding (chapter three), but also to fast with humility and prayerfulness. That will be the focus of this book's fourth chapter, as we consider how fasting takes us to our knees.

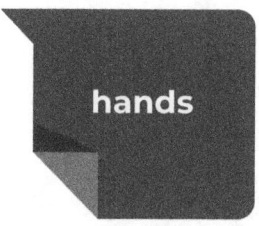

- fasting can be for just one meal, or many
- when you fast drink lots of water
- always link fasting with prayer
- prepare well before fasting and gather resources
- end your fast with a feast, with others if you can

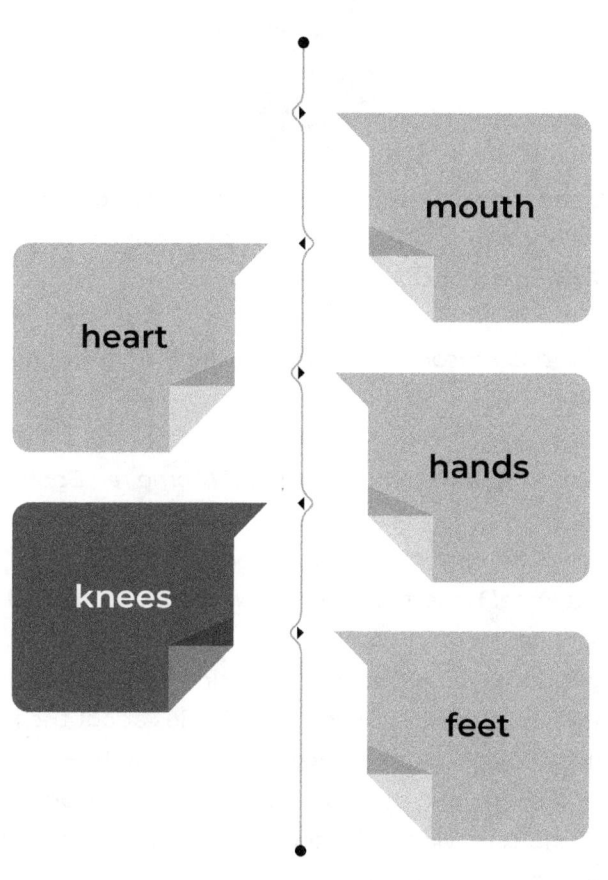

Chapter 4

- *'... at the name of Jesus every knee should bow ... and every tongue acknowledge that Jesus Christ is Lord' (Philippians 2:10).*

- *'For this reason I kneel before the Father' (Ephesians 3:14).*

- *'A man is powerful on his knees' (Corrie ten Boom).*[1]

- *'Humility honors God, and God honors humility. Why not kneel? It certainly can't hurt' (Mark Batterson).*[2]

Hegesippus was a story-teller. Writing in the second century AD, he especially liked to recall tales about the heroic exploits of leaders in the first-century church. He enjoyed writing so much that he scribed a five-volume account in the simplest style for the ordinary person to understand, known today as Hegesippus' *Hypomnemata*. This very early history of the church was a great asset to Christians in the first centuries, both verifying and filling out many accounts of events and people that we read about today in the New Testament and also in the writings of the initial followers of Jesus. But there's a problem. We can't enjoy or analyse Hegesippus' work any more, for there are no known surviving copies. We can only appreciate his writing today through the Christian historian Eusebius, who had a copy of *Hypomnemata* in front of him as he wrote two centuries later.

Eusebius particularly relied on Hegesippus when he described James, the brother of Jesus. Often known as James the Just, this James was probably the writer of *The Epistle of James* which appears towards the end of the New Testament. Hegesippus describes a number of things about James, including the fact that he practised a permanent *Alcohol Fast* as well as *Daniel Fast*. But the most memorable thing about James was his nickname, which Eusebius learned from *Hypomnemata*, saying that James was known as 'Old Camel Knees'! Here's why. James was a person of deep and devoted prayer, with Hegesippus saying that he 'was frequently found upon his knees begging forgiveness for the people, so that his knees became hard like those of a camel, in consequence of his constantly bending them in his worship of God, and asking forgiveness'.[3] It seems that James the Just developed thick calluses which built up on his knees. It was probably evidence of many years of determined fasting and humble prayer.

This fourth chapter of *The Art of Fasting* is all about humility, particularly expressed by bowing the knee in prayer. It describes one of the most important aspects of Christian fasting, which is that it helps us prayerfully and reverently seek God and his kingdom reign. The chapter is not so much about fasting for God to change *us*, as we've considered that in chapter two, rather it's more that he'll change people, places and circumstances. It's about kneeling in intercession for all sorts of situations, humbly crying out to God as we recognise that 'Prayer moves the hand that moves the world.'[4]

Methodism

Looking back in history, one tradition of the church from which we learn much about this kind of intercessory fasting, is Methodism. John Wesley, the founder of the Methodist movement, taught that 'God will hearken to the prayer that goeth not out of feigned lips; especially when fasting is joined therewith.'[5] Wesley not only modelled prayerful fasting to his people but spoke about it often, encouraging the practice as foundational to discipleship and mission. He would regularly fast before major personal decisions, in preparation for church conferences, to identify with the poor and before ordinations, and at the end of the year he would fast during the annual 'watch-night service', in preparation for the coming year. He did all this not as a means of his own salvation, for he knew that had been won by Christ on the cross, but rather because he believed that fasting empowered prayer, saying that 'When two or three agree to seek God by fasting and prayer, it cannot be that their labour should be in vain.'[6]

Lee Roy Martin, in his historical study on fasting, concludes that John Wesley 'taught that fasting was beneficial for many reasons, but the chief benefit was as an aid to prayer'.[7] That is why, in this chapter, we will consider four humble and prayerful reasons for fasting, many of which have been seen in the Methodist movement.

1) Release

First, we fast to ask God to *release* his power into all sorts of situations. Some people find this hard to understand. Why should something that makes us weak, actually produce strength? How does something that could produce death, actually bring life? It seems not only counterintuitive but unreasonable. The answer is best articulated by analogy, explaining what fasting is like.

Fasting is like yeast, activating dough and setting it growing. Fasting is like a catalyst, causing elements to react and releasing fresh energy. Fasting is like an accelerator, triggering an engine to advance at a faster pace. This is surely one reason why Jesus fasted before he began his public ministry. Of course, he wanted to stand firm against the tempting voice of the evil one, and no doubt he desired to become even more disciplined in his prayer habits, but most of all he wanted to see God's power released, changing lives and situations for good. He longed for the experience he had of the Holy Spirit at his baptism to be channelled to serve God's kingdom and to help others,[8] which is exactly what happened after Jesus fasted. Not only that, but later on in his ministry, Jesus delivered a young boy from an evil spirit which his disciples couldn't expel. When asked how, Jesus replied in Mark 9:29, 'This kind can come out only by prayer [and fasting].' Some Bible translations exclude 'and fasting' as a number of early manuscripts don't include those two words, but whether Jesus actually said them or not, their inclusion shows many of the earliest churches believed he did, convinced that prayer on its own was often insufficient to see the breakthrough that was needed. It required prayer *and* fasting! Founder of Methodism John Wesley agreed, teaching his followers that certain matters, including various medical conditions were beyond the reach of medics, and change would only come with prayer and fasting.[9] Why? Because fasting releases the power of God.

This means that it's often helpful to have a target when we fast. I've found that's not necessary all the time, for as we've seen, it's sometimes good just to fast as a sign of humble devotion and to open our hearts to God. However, there are also many times when I need to fast *for* a particular person or situation. They become my prayer focus as I fast. The Bible has multiple examples of this. Here are a few, describing how people fasted when praying for:

- *protection from opposition:* as Jehoshaphat did (in 2 Chronicles 20:3-4) when he heard a vast army was coming against them.
- *safety while travelling:* like Ezra did before making a long and potentially hazardous journey (Ezra 8:21–23).
- *guidance for the future:* the Israelites fasted in the time of war between the tribes, in the context of sadness and worship, as they sought God's will going ahead (Judges 20:26).
- *change when grieving:* as David and his men did (in 2 Samuel 1:12) after the death of Saul and Jonathan, expressing regret and remorse, and wanting to see transformation.
- *repentance from sin:* like the Israelites did (in 1 Samuel 7:6) recognising their rebellious hearts and confessing their sin to God.[10]
- *healing from illness:* David sometimes fasted, asking for healing (see Psalm 35:13 and 2 Samuel 12:16).
- *deliverance from evil:* as Jesus did when delivering a demonised boy (Mark 9:29) and extensively when oppressed by demonic temptation (Matthew 4:1–11).

- *choosing new leaders:* the apostles fasted before selecting elders for the first churches (Acts 13:1–4; 14:23).
- *success in mission:* the church in Antioch was fasting when God called them to send out Barnabas and Saul to plant churches. They continued to fast, not only to confirm the word but also seeking God's success in the missionary endeavour to which they were called (see Acts 13:2–3).

Aware of these biblical examples, Lou Engle says that when he fasts, he finds it helpful to 'have a clear target for prayer', noting that 'During a fast I often pray into four or five prayer goals, but I must make sure that they are clearly articulated. When I'm not deeply motivated by a clear goal, I usually fast until break-fast!'[11] I have done the same over the years, fasting for all sorts of things. At The Belfrey in York, which I led before becoming a bishop, we would often suggest a focus when we invited the church to fast. For example, we have fasted for various breakthroughs, for encounter with God, for evangelistic breakthrough and for lifestyle change as people grasp the serious nature of the present climate crisis.

2) Revive

Second, we intercede with fasting, asking the Lord to *revive* his church, so God's people overflow with his Spirit and are sent out as Christ's missionary disciples in the world. Jennifer Miskov is a researcher in revival history. Her interest in the subject has led her to write not only in the fields of history and leadership but also in spirituality and fasting, becoming convinced that 'Fasting is a key for pioneering revival.'[12] She recognises this begins by being dissatisfied not only with the state of the *world* but with the state of the *church*, recognising the need for God to come and intervene, saying: 'In my studies of revival history over the last several decades, *the number-one attribute that is present in the beginnings of almost every revival I've looked at is hunger.*'[13] People realise their need of divine help and so pray that God would begin by reviving them, crying out in prayer: 'Send revival, start with me.'

As I read the Scriptures, I see there are many times when God's people in the Old Testament lose their bearings, neglect their heritage and forget to prioritise prayer and care for those in need. At such times prophets often emerge, calling people back to God. The prophets are often supported by intercessors, praying for hearts to turn back to God, buoyed by God's words to Solomon in 2 Chronicles 7:14: 'if my people, who are called by my name, will humble themselves and pray and seek my face and turn from their wicked ways, then I will hear from heaven, and I will forgive their sin and will heal their land.' The pattern of church history since Pentecost is not dissimilar, with God's Spirit awakening his church when it is struggling or corrupt or divided, and in particular, when it has lost its missional focus, often aided by prophetic voices and prayerful saints. That's why evangelist D.L. Moody rightly said, 'Every move of God can be traced to a kneeling figure.'[14] Often these intercessors are praying that God would ignite his people, setting them on fire with love for Christ and compassion for his world. If we want a church on fire, we need to fast.

I have fasted a number of times specifically for revival in the church. Sometimes this is for local revival in my own church and city, asking the Lord to pour out his Spirit upon us in a fresh and dynamic way. I know of a number of church leaders who have done this, including Paul Lowe of the Manchester Vineyard. He told me recently that five days after he'd called his church to a season of fasting, the school building in which they met on Sundays had a fire and had to close. This resulted in many in the church praying and seeking God with greater intensity for a new venue. The leaders contacted more than seventy venues before finding the one they believed was right. When they announced where, a number of those who'd been fasting said they already knew! They'd been prayer-walking and sensed the Spirit point out that very building that was to be their new home. Since then, the church has continued to grow and make further plans for planting. This all came in a season of prayer with fasting, asking the Lord for revival.

Knees

I've also fasted a few times in the past for national revival, and sometimes done this while joining in with various national prayer initiatives. While it's impossible to measure the effectiveness of such times, I know they are good and important and transformational. Writing this section in this book has convicted me that in recent years I have neglected fasting for *national* revival, and now that I am a bishop in the church, which includes a national brief, this is something I know I must do more.

Rees Howells (1879–1950) is a fascinating example of a revivalist and intercessor. Finding personal faith in Christ in a Methodist chapel when in Montana in the USA, he returned to Wales fired up and was part of what today is known as The Welsh Revival of 1904–05, seeing many find faith in Christ and enlivened by the Spirit.[15] His life was marked by intersession and by a prayerfulness that many found compelling, later being a great example to Norman Grubb who led the Worldwide Evangelization Crusade (WEC – an organisation which my parents supported for many decades) and causing Grubb to write Howell's biography in 1967. During one season of his life, Grubb records that Howells fasted two meals a day, and during this time he also spent three hours every night on his knees in prayer each evening. He fasted for breakthrough in all sorts of areas, including that the expansive plans of dictators would be thwarted and peace experienced, and sometimes when fasting he sensed the Holy Spirit give him strategies to employ in his life and work. But in the end Howells fasted mainly to pray for revival: for personal revival for himself and his family, and most of all for the wider sake of revival in his native Wales, in the UK and beyond.

3) Renewal

Third, we fast with prayer, calling out for God to *renew* society, praying that contemporary life becomes more kind, just and generous, infused by the presence of Christ. While 'renewal' is a term which Christians have sometimes used of God's Spirit reinvigorating the church, I am using it here more expansively, as a descriptor of his work beyond the church and bringing wider social and cultural change. This is a kingdom-of-God vision, of God's reign coming on earth as it is in heaven, which is what Jesus told us in Matthew 6:10 to pray for daily, in the Lord's Prayer. Clearly this kind of transformation comes through much practical action, but Christ-followers believe it also occurs through prayerful fasting. Jennifer Miskov is helpful here, pointing out that 'Fasting is a sign of our inability to effect the change needed in our society apart from [God's] grace.'[16]

This kind of fasting requires faith and perseverance, as we call out to God for the world he loves so much. Those who fast for this often find themselves praying for peace in war-torn parts of the world, as I've been doing recently as I have initiated *#prayforpeacewednesday*. When fasting in early 2024 I sensed a growing tug on my heart to pray for peace in areas of the world where things felt stuck, especially in the terrible conflicts in Ukraine and in Gaza/Israel. I then received an email from a woman called Clare, asking if, as a bishop, I would begin to lead some prayers for this. I sensed this wasn't a coincidence and was a prophetic call and so, having talked with my prayer partners, I began *#prayforpeacewednesdays,* praying weekly for an end to conflict in war-torn parts of the world. Not many know that the catalyst for this was prayer with fasting. While some may consider it preposterous that our prayers can make any difference on a global scale, followers of Christ have always believed they can, with the *Didache*, written around AD 100, saying: 'pray for your enemies, and fast for those who persecute you',[17] convinced that fasting can help change the hearts of even belligerent people. Basil the Great goes further, saying: 'if all were to take fasting as the counsellor for their actions, nothing would prevent a profound peace from spreading throughout the entire world.'[18] Rees Howells, as we have seen, is another example of an intercessor who fasted for world peace and for the greater good of society. And John Wesley was the same, seeking for the renewal of British society, asking in the so-called 'Large' Minutes of Methodism: 'What may we reasonably believe to be God's design in raising up the

Preachers called Methodists? To reform the nation and, in particular, the Church; to spread scriptural holiness over the land.'[19] Wesley expressed this vision through his work, and particularly through regular prayer and fasting.

4) Return

A fourth reason to prayerfully fast is for the *return* of Christ, praying that his second coming would come soon. The Lord came for a first time, wonderfully and decisively 2,000 years ago in the person of Jesus Christ, and he has promised to come again. His first coming changed the world, so much so that our ancestors redated time on his coming; his second coming will end time. As we live in what theologians call 'an eschatological tension' between these two comings, we are called through our actions and our prayers to encourage this. According to Scot McKnight, the early church believed this was important, fasting 'because they longed for Christ to return to establish the kingdom of God'.[20] John Piper agrees, saying, 'Fasting is a physical expression of heart-hunger for the coming of Jesus.'[21]

Those who fast in this way look back and look ahead. They look back to the feasting that the disciples enjoyed in the presence of Christ and to his sacrificial death on the cross, remembered every time the Lord's Supper is shared, and they look forward to the great banquet in heaven that will be enjoyed in the full presence of Christ, with his saints in glory. In this in-between time they fast and say, 'Come Lord Jesus,' welcoming his final return and even, in some kind of mysterious and wonderful way, speeding it through their lives and prayerful fasts,[22] inviting people to kneel before Christ now, in anticipation of the day in eternity when, according to Philippians 2:10, 'at the name of Jesus every knee should bow'. This is a rarely mentioned aspect of fasting that I have not focused on in the past, but I now will.

Decline

There are many other humble reasons why followers of Jesus prayerfully fast – and this chapter has mentioned just four of the main ones. Central to all this is the belief by Christ-followers that fasting humbles us to our knees in prayer, being a lowly and prayerful holy habit which helps release God's power. As we have seen in this chapter, Wesley and the early Methodists sincerely believed this, and it seems that while they practised this discipline, along with other key habits like meeting in small groups for accountability and discipleship, so the Methodist movement grew and multiplied. But as these holy habits in time became more optional, so the movement started to lose some of its fire, momentum began to slow and the seeds of decline set in.[23] John Wesley had founded the Methodist movement not only on evangelism and church planting, but on disciplined discipleship, being highly influenced by the church fathers of the early centuries of the church.

He called the fathers 'the most authentic commentators on scriptures' and said 'I exceedingly reverence them.'[24] Wesley regularly read their writings, including that of John Chrysostom, who said:

> Fasting is, as much as lies in us, an imitation of the angels, a contemning of things present, a school of prayer, a nourishments of the soul, a bridle of the mouth, and abatement of concupiscence: it mollifies rage, it appeases anger, it calms the tempests of nature, it excites reasons, it clears the mind, it disburdens the flesh, it excites reason, it clears the mind, it disburdens the flesh, it chases away night-pollutions, it frees from head-ache. By fasting, a man gets composed behaviour, free utterance of his tongue, right apprehensions of his mind.[25]

Chrysostom was clearly a fasting fan! He was a passionate advocate of humble fasting who, when offering a variety of reasons for fasting, notably begins with *angels*. So it's with angels that we close this chapter.

Angels

The understanding that angels are present and assist when we fast is an ancient one. It goes back to Christ himself who, while fasting in the wilderness 'angels came and attended him'.[26] If we dig deeper, we see that hundreds of years before Christ, the prophet Daniel had fasted and prayed, and then Michael the archangel spoke with him, telling him, 'Since the first day that you set your mind to gain understanding and to humble yourself before your God, your words were heard, and I have come in response to them.'[27] And before that Elijah had fasted, and twice an angel 'touched him', spoke with him and provided for him.[28] We have already seen in chapter two that angels are often at work when we repent and turn our hearts to God, as we seek to be refined by the fire of his love. We've also noted that Basil the Great believed that 'Fasting sends prayer up to heaven, as if it were its wings for the upward journey'[29] but so far this book has not said how. The answer, says Basil, is by angels.

Basil thought angels were intricately involved in fasting, saying that it is 'the angels who diligently guard our life [and] stand beside those who purify their soul through fasting'.[30] Building on the teaching of John Chrysostom, who said that fasting 'is an extraordinarily powerful thing. It makes us mortals into angels',[31] Basil the Great believed that when we mix prayer with fasting we are becoming angel-like, for 'fasting is the likeness of angels'[32] which is a view held by all Abrahamic faiths today.[33] Not only this, but Basil also thought that when we feast on God's Word while fasting, the angels assist.[34] Basil was such a supporter of fasting that he urged churches to keep a register of those who fasted, considering there to be one in heaven, held by the angels. This explains why he said, 'No one should remove himself from the register of those who fast, in which all peoples and all ages and all ranks of dignity are counted. It is angels who register them in each church.'[35]

Down the centuries there's been a long tradition teaching that fasting is supported by angels, and this belief has been revived in recent years by the teaching of some Pentecostal Christians, the tradition we will consider in our next and final chapter.[36] I welcome this understanding of angelic support for fasting, as long as the main focus is on Christ, for he is the King of the angels[37] and the One the angels serve, and all fasting and praying should be in his name. Fasting is not about kneeling before angels but kneeling before Christ. It's choosing not to eat food, with a prayerful and humble heart, recognising with Pete Greig, that 'The rusty hinge of human history turns out to be the bended knee.'[38]

Having discussed *the hunger* behind fasting (chapter one); *the desire* of fasting (chapter two); *the practicalities* of fasting (chapter three) and *the intercession* of fasting (chapter four), in our final chapter we'll consider *the mission* of fasting, seeing fasting as central to God's outreach plans into which we're called.

knees

- fasting humbles us
- fasting helps us to pray
- fasting releases the power of God
- fasting brings revival and renewal
- fasting is supported by angels

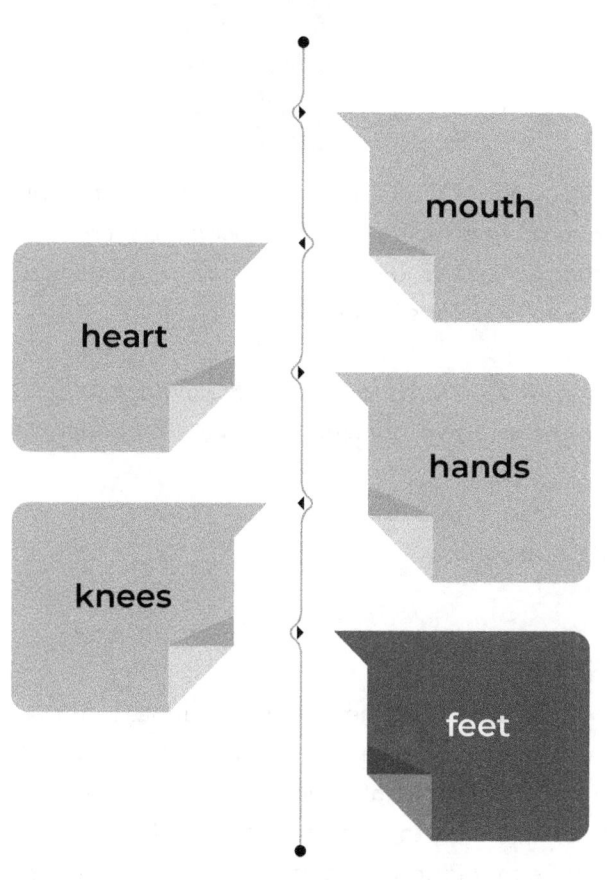

Chapter 5

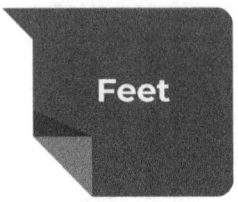
Feet

- *'How beautiful on the mountains are the feet of those who bring good news, who proclaim peace, who bring good tidings, who proclaim salvation, who say to Zion, "Your God reigns!"' (Isaiah 52:7).*

- *'"Make level paths for your feet," so that the lame may not be disabled, but rather healed' (Hebrews 12:13).*

- *'Solvitur ambulando – It is solved by walking' (St Augustine).*[1]

- *'We write history with our feet' (Rebecca Solnit).*[2]

In March 1965 at the height of civil rights tension in the USA, Nobel Peace Prize winner, the Revd Dr Martin Luther King Jr. led a series of peaceful marches from Selma in Alabama, aiming to reach the state capital of Montgomery some fifty-four miles away. The marches were to draw attention to racial discrimination, for while voting for black people was now legal in the state, the process of registering to vote was all but impossible for them, effectively disenfranchising all but white people. The marches have gone down in history as pivotal moments in the civil rights struggle, with the first resulting in brutal beatings of peaceful walkers, the second stalling, but the third successfully reaching Montgomery on 25th March where numbers swelled to nearly 50,000 people who heard King and other prominent speakers address the crowd, declaring, 'No tide of racism can stop us!' What, however, is sometimes missed in the retelling is the prayer. At times King would ask the marchers to pause and kneel in the street in humble prayer. All the marches began in prayer. Many people prayed while they walked. And some of those walking not only prayed but did so with hungry stomachs, choosing to walk while fasting.[3]

One of the crowd who marched from Selma, walking at the very front of the line, was legendary Jewish cleric and friend of Dr King, Rabbi Abraham Joshua Heschel. He was pleased to walk with King, to stand for justice, and to link humble prayer with practical action. When Rabbi Heschel returned from Selma, he was asked by someone, 'Did you find much time to pray, when you were in Selma?' Rabbi Heschel's response was short and telling, declaring, 'I prayed with my feet.'[4]

It's easy to forget that the civil rights movement of the 1960s, like many movements for change down the centuries, was immersed in prayer and fasting. But King and Heschel knew that for true transformation to take place, their prayers needed to be expressed not only through their mouths and on their knees, but also through their feet. This final chapter of *The Art of Fasting* is all about feet. As we consider more of why and how the body-prayer of fasting is powerful and effective, we will pick up Rabbi Heschel's response, who himself was unknowingly echoing a phrase of the fourth-century church father John Chrysostom who said, 'Let the feet fast,'[5] recognising there's a bigger and grander purpose for fasting. Fasting is not just to make us more healthy and more holy; it's meant to change the world.

Uncovered

Someone whose feet were used to change the world was Moses. He lived around 1400 BC in Egypt at a time, not unlike that of King Jr., when his people had become slaves to the indigenous population. While tending his family's flock one day, he came across a bush on fire which wouldn't burn up. It got his attention, and as he investigated an angel of the Lord appeared. The encounter was deeply revolutionary for him, for out of the fire he heard the voice of God calling, 'Moses! Moses!' He was told the place on which he was standing was sacred and that he should take off his sandals. Despite feeling unworthy in God's holy presence and hiding his face, the voice continued, telling

Moses that God had seen the injustice done to the people of Israel in Egypt and that Moses was now being sent to liberate them.[6]

The missionary task to which Moses was called was not easy. He lacked courage and needed help, which would require much prayer and fasting. But it also included action. This action was expressed in feet, as God's people literally walked out of Egypt. But it began with Moses' *bare* feet, responding to the holy presence of God. They were naked, vulnerable feet, respectfully exposed before God. Moses' bare feet represent the posture of the heart we considered in chapter two, reflecting an open and uncovered disposition before the Holy One, reverent and consecrated in his hallowed presence. This is always the starting point of effective action, for missional feet must first be holy feet. Before you put your shoes on, you have to take them off.

Cleansed

About seven hundred years later, the prophet Isaiah had an encounter with God where he too was called to mission. We considered it in chapter two, for it changed his heart. It began with a powerful vision of the grandeur of God and has some similarities to Moses' calling, for it also involved angels appearing, fire burning and a profound experience of divine holiness, out of which God spoke and Isaiah was commissioned. Like Moses, Isaiah also felt initially unworthy in God's presence, declaring 'Woe to me! . . . I am a man of unclean lips' but he was wonderfully transformed as an angel touched his lips with a burning coal, cleansing his heart.

While there is no record of him removing his shoes, the experience began with Isaiah's mouth, went through his heart and effected his feet, for when he heard the Lord's voice asking, 'Whom shall I send? And who will go for us?' Isaiah responded, 'Here am I. Send me!'[7] Like Moses, Isaiah discovered that cleansing births calling. An experience of holiness that doesn't produce mission hasn't gone far enough, for it's meant to commission us to impact the world, sending us out with holy feet.

Humbled

Travel on another 700 years and we find Jesus, at the height of his ministry, telling his disciples to take off their shoes so he can wash their feet. Wrapping a towel round his waist, Jesus pours water into a basin and one by one he cleans off the dirt of the day, and then dries their feet with a towel. The writer of John's Gospel who records the account in 13:1–17 makes little comment of the disciples' reaction except for that of Peter, who rather like Moses and Elijah before him feels unworthy and seems reluctant to be washed. In response, Jesus tells Peter that the disciples must have their feet washed and allow this cleansing to impact the whole of their lives. As the story unfolds it becomes clear that Peter's reluctance isn't just sensing unworthiness in the presence of divinity, for he's already well acquainted with that feeling,[8] but comes more from knowing that foot-washing in his culture was a job for a lowest servant, not a master. That in the end becomes Jesus' main point, telling his followers, 'Now that I, your Lord and Teacher, have washed your feet, you also should wash one another's feet,'[9] showing that discipleship is about service, and that leadership requires deep humility. Jesus then modelled this for them like no other, by dying the slave's death on a cross, sacrificing his very life for them.

I wrote a short reflection about this episode recently for the Diocese of Manchester's Prayer Community, and said this:

> Not everyone likes their feet. But Jesus was happy to take his followers' feet in his hands and gently and lovingly wash them. Such a physical, intimate and (for some) uncomfortable expression of servanthood is hard to find. But it goes further. It's a sign of closeness. It's a sign of cleansing. It's a sign of caring. But don't forget it's also a sign of commissioning, for feet signify 'going' as we're sent out as Christ's missionary disciples, shaped by the liberating good news of Easter.

This significant story about feet tells us that Jesus, the Holy One, gladly takes hold of our grubby lives, and gently and purposefully washes us. He wants us to be holy like him, to be servant-hearted like him, and to have a missional passion like him, and so he illustrates all this in one simple act, of washing feet. *Feet*, of all things! Smelly feet. Tired feet. Knobbly feet. Scarred feet. Sensitive feet. What he does is intimate without being erotic, and deeply personal without being introspective, for by choosing feet, Jesus' followers would have known that in Jewish tradition they signified 'going'. Like Moses and Elijah before them, the disciples were being shown that cleansing and commissioning go together, and that truly missional leadership is humble leadership.

Ambassadors

As we've been discovering in this book, one of the main ways we are trained in this kind of humility is through learning *The Art of Fasting*. It's both a response to the holiness of God and, when practised intentionally and regularly, is a means of us becoming holy, like God. But more than this, it's meant to propel us out in mission, as people with servant hearts who are ambassadors for Christ in word and action. If it doesn't do this, it's only doing half its work, *inside* of us; the other half is meant to be *outside* of us, as we serve God's mission in the world.

The Anglican tradition has many things to teach us about fasting, but it's often missed fasting's missional dimension. John Jewel, for example, who wrote *Of Good Works: and*

First of Fasting in 1571, shaped much Anglican thinking on the subject and speaks of fasting having three aims: first 'to chastise the flesh', second 'that [we] may be more fervent and earnest in prayer' and third 'that our fast may be a testimony and witness with us before God of our humble submission to his high Majesty'.[10] When I first read this, I assumed that Jewel's third reason, about 'testimony and witness' was about impacting *people* with the gospel, but a closer reading shows it is about showing to *God* the seriousness of our devotion. While there is some value in this, it misses the point of this final chapter, that fasting is supposed to produce a strong missionary heart in us, causing both our prayers and our actions to be more missionally effective towards *others*. For Anglicans like me to learn of this, we need to especially find inspiration in other traditions, and the one that has helped us see this more than most in recent years is Pentecostalism.

Pentecostalism

Historians of mission tell us that the most impactful missionary movement in the church of the last century has undoubtedly come from the Pentecostal churches. Today the movement stands at almost 600,000 million adherents, making up about 27 per cent of Christians and representing more than 8 per cent of the world's population.[11] In telling the story of Pentecostal growth, missiologists sometimes miss that Pentecostalism was birthed not only in prayer but in fasting, with the first leaders greatly shaped in spirituality by the Wesleyan tradition that we considered in chapter four. Pentecostals trace the birth of their movement to events at the Azusa Street Mission in Los Angeles in 1906 but it's easily forgotten that a group had been praying for about a year for revival beforehand. They then called William Seymour to lead them who, according to *Apostolic Faith* magazine, invited them to 'fast and pray for the baptism of the Holy Spirit, till on April 9th the fire of God fell'.[12] The same was true of the Pentecostal experience that ignited the Church of God (Cleveland), where in 1907 the people 'prayed, fasted and wept before the Lord until a great revival was the result'.[13]

Lee Roy Martin has researched further, and notes that fasting was central to the genesis of the Pentecostal movement, saying that their first leaders 'adopted fasting as an important practice' and he goes on to describe 'more than 50 reports of fasting that I have uncovered in the early literature, about half refer to individual fasting, and about half refer to corporate fasting'[14] and that they fasted both for themselves and for others. He describes how this was less about following a liturgical calendar and more about need, and that fasts lasted from one to fourteen days and often involved foot-washing. While fasting some, including children, had profound encounters with Jesus, others experienced healing, and a minority went to excess – which was harshly rebuked by leaders – with a few sadly dying of starvation. Martin summarises his study by saying that 'In early Pentecostalism, fasting was utilized as an aid to any kind of urgent prayer, especially when pleading for revival and the salvation of lost souls',[15] with early Pentecostal Pearl Page Brown of the Church of God of Christ asserting that 'Prayer and fasting go together to penetrate and to break through every resistance that the enemy has built. Fasting strengthens and intensifies our prayers.'[16] It is noteworthy that where Pentecostalism is growing across the world today, as we see in many African and Indian communities, it is usually marked by prayer and fasting. Indeed, in my book *The A–Z of Discipleship*, I reference the words of a Nigerian pastor who, when asked why the church in the UK was not experiencing the growth and outpouring of the Spirit that they were seeing, replied, 'You don't know how to pray and fast.'[17]

Planting

There are, however, some signs of growth in today's UK church, usually in communities that are committed to mission and seeing a movement of church planting in their region. When undertaking my doctoral research on church planting in 2019, I was keen to understand these movements and the spirituality behind them, so I choose ten leaders of growing Western church-planting movements, examining the personal prayer life of their leaders and the corporate prayer life of the movements. As well as recognising that these leaders and their churches were envisioned by a missional mindset, a number of significant and perhaps surprising common findings emerged with regard to prayer, including:

- church planting movements are fuelled by rhythms of *regular prayer*
  (with leaders praying daily every morning, and their churches praying weekly)
- church planting movements are sustained by *passionate petition*
  (with leaders and their churches using various forms of prayer, especially intercession)
- church planting movements are catalysed by *faithful fasting*
  (with leaders and churches using a variety of prayer practices, with all fasting).[18]

Although limited in its scope, this research is telling. It shows that the church planting leaders are praying leaders, and that church planting churches are praying churches. It concurs with historical studies of renewal movements, which show that prayer is central.[19] Not only this, it shows that *fasting* is a central prayer practice of all these renewal leaders and their growing churches. This research has not yet been written up in popular form, and would benefit from a wider and more comprehensive study in the future to test its finding, but I share it here in summary form, as it suggests, as this chapter on fasting is arguing, that fasting and missionary impact go together.

Leadership

While my doctoral research was on the *prayer* behind the church planting movements, it also unashamedly focused on *leadership*, wanting to explore the influence of leaders, not only on the growth of their churches but on the church's spirituality. Its findings mirrored anecdotal and empirical evidence showing that organisations are not only shaped by leaders but also tend to take on the characteristics of the senior leader – both the good and the not so good.[20] This means that if we want our churches to be generous, it helps to have a leader who's generous. If we want our churches to be praying, it's good to have a leader who prays. And if we want our churches to fast, it's best to have a leader who fasts.

Leaders lead. It's their job. They lead by both word and example. If we believe that holy habits are important, as this *Art of* . . . series does (following Aquinas and others), then spiritual disciplines need to be practised and taught by leaders. This is probably best modelled for us in today's churches by many *Pentecostal* leaders. But as we go back through church history, it has also been exemplified well in leaders of all the traditions we have explored. John Wesley, as we have seen, fasted regularly, and said that the leaders in *Methodism* should fast for two days each week as part of their regular rhythm of worship and devotion. In fact, people could not be considered for ordination by Wesley if they did not fast in this way. While *Anglican* divines at the Reformation rejected the Roman Catholic assertion that fasting brought salvation, they still taught that fasting was important and should be practised and led by the clergy. Thomas Becon, the Anglican priest who wrote a significant pamphlet entitled *A Fruitful Treatise of Fasting* in 1551, expressed concern in the Preface for 'negligent Prelates and sleepy shepherds, which watch not over the Lord's flock', saying that fasting was important for 'all men that tender the glory of God, but specially the Lord's Ministers'.[21] *Orthodox* church leaders have also encouraged the practice among their clergy, with Basil the Great saying, 'it is impossible to venture upon priestly activities without fasting'.[22] The *Catholic* tradition has likewise done the same, urging its priests to set a good example by keeping regular fasts, including before the Eucharist, with Augustine of Hippo teaching that 'It was pleasing to the Holy Spirit that, out of reverence for this great Sacrament, the Body of the Lord should enter the mouth of the Christian before any other food.'[23]

Before choosing leaders, the church has often fasted, learning from Christ himself, who prayed all night on a mountainside – presumably fasting – before next morning calling his disciples to follow him.[24] According to Luke, the author of Luke-Acts, Paul and Barnabas used this approach on their first missionary journey as they appointed elders 'in each church and, with prayer and fasting, committed them to the Lord, in whom they had put their trust'.[25] It seems that fasting helped them as they prayerfully discerned all the matters around appointing leaders, and most importantly, *who* should be appointed. I have often prayed with fasting when considering a new role for myself, and also when appointing significant leaders to a church team. Just this week, while writing this chapter, a church leader from Sheffield told me that a colleague joining them had fasted for many days before submitting their job application, seeking clarity on whether they were being sent by the Holy Spirit.

Spirit

One of the marks of Pentecostalism and their leaders has been, and is, their dependency on the Holy Spirit, relying on his presence and power not only for their own salvation and sanctification, but for the church's ongoing mission. They know that when they pray with fasting, they see more of the Spirit's work. Like other traditions of the church, they realise this is not a mechanical process and that there is something of a mystery to this, but in the end they know it's true. So they fast.

In many ways this should not surprise us, for God's creative empowering presence – the Holy Spirit – is missionary in nature, and wants to impact our feet. He is 'Holy' and other. He is God. He wants to make us holy like him. When we stand in his presence and encounter his holiness, we are exposed and this is sometimes expressed through taking off our shoes. And yet he is also 'Spirit'. He is God's creative, free-flowing, liberating presence who moves and touches and heals and transforms, bringing God's kingdom not just to us, but through us to others. So, he invites us to sandal-up and go! Jesus' final words to his disciples before his resurrection are all about this, saying: 'you will receive power when the Holy Spirit comes on you; and you will be my witnesses.'[26] Shoes off soon becomes shoes on, and it's often while fasting that this occurs, as the Spirit who empowers becomes the Spirit who sends.

As the first disciples sought this power from the Spirit after the ascension of Jesus, what did they do? Luke tells us in Acts that they gathered in an upstairs room and 'all joined together constantly in prayer'.[27] We're not told if they fasted, but it's likely that they did, especially as one of their first tasks was to choose a leader to replace Judas. They continued like this for ten days until, on the Jewish feast day of Pentecost, while praying and 'all together in one place . . . All of them were filled with the Holy Spirit' and propelled outside, 'declaring the wonders of God' in a variety of languages, bubbling out with missional energy and joy, birthing the church and seeing many lives transformed.[28] This was the work of the missionary Holy Spirit then, and the same Holy Spirit is at work today, empowering and sending out people who pray and fast.

The founding fathers of early Pentecostalism, living in an age when there was much neglect of fasting, sincerely taught that the discipline of fasting was crucial for releasing God's powerful Spirit for mission. For example, Samuel C. Perry of the Church of God wrote an article in 1915 stating that 'there are blessings and decrees sometimes that seem to be out of our reach except through fasting and prayer',[29] and I believe he's right. Perhaps one reason why the church in the West seems often so powerless and lacking in the presence of God's Spirit, is our neglect of humble prayer with fasting.

Sent

In the early days of the church, when this Holy Spirit spoke powerfully and prophetically to the church in Antioch and made it clear that Barnabas and Saul should be sent out to plant churches in the region, the encounter took place while the people were fasting. Acts 13:2–3 describes the scene, saying that while the Antioch leaders were spending time in God's holy presence 'worshipping the Lord and fasting' that 'the Holy Spirit said, "Set apart for me Barnabas and Saul for the work to which I have called them".' In response, the leaders tested the message with more fasting and prayer before 'they placed their hands on them and sent them off'. Once again it was through fasting that holy feet became missional feet.

It seems that every time fasting is mentioned positively in the New Testament, it has some kind of missionary consequence. Here are some examples:

- *Matthew 4:1–12* Jesus fasts, is tempted and overcomes Satan by God's Word, is attended by angels, and then immediately goes to Nazareth to declare God's kingdom, inviting people to follow him.
- *Matthew 6:16–18* Jesus teaches on fasting in the Sermon on the Mount, which produces rewards not for us to keep, but to give away and share with others.
- *Matthew 9:15* Jesus says his disciples will fast after his death and resurrection, as they declare and preach the message of the cross.
- *Matthew 17:21* Jesus says that prayer and fasting are necessary before some forms of transformation can take place.
- *Luke 2:37–38* Anna, the prophet who fasts, meets the infant Jesus and his parents, and she is overjoyed, thanking God and telling everyone about him.
- *Acts 9ff* Paul fasts after discovering to his surprise that Christ really is the Messiah, and is alive.

He's subsequently filled with the Holy Spirit and at once begins to preach about Christ.

- *Acts 10:30ff* As Cornelius, a Roman centurion, fasts and prays, an angel appears and tells him to find Peter, who helps him find faith.
- *Acts 13:2–3* As the Antioch church fasts, so Barnabas and Saul are called and sent out to evangelise and plant churches.
- *Acts 14:23* Paul and Barnabas fast and appoint elders, freeing the apostles to continue in their regional mission while the newly appointed leaders serve locally.
- *Acts 27:33–34* Paul urges sailors to end their fast, in order to save him and all onboard the ship.
- *2 Corinthians 6:3–10* Paul declares that he has been through all sorts of hardships, including fasting, in order to speak freely of Christ.
- *2 Corinthians 11:27* Paul again lists all sorts of difficulties, including going without food, in order to boast about the strength of God which is released through him to others.

The New Testament shows, then, that fasting always has a bigger missional intent. That was the case 2,000 years ago and should still be the same today. Lee Roy Martin, who at the end of his study on fasting declares that he is a minister in the Pentecostal church, recognises this, saying,

'Fasting should produce in the leader a dependency upon the Lord and upon his Holy Spirit',[30] having himself 'witnessed revivals, healings, miracles, the working of spiritual gifts, the resolution of church conflicts, and divine guidance in response to fasting and prayer'.[31] Along with other Pentecostal leaders, Martin encourages both disciples and leaders to fast, not only because the habit is taught in the Scriptures but because fasting has always been at the heart of spiritual awakening in church history, and particularly in Pentecostalism, with an early record of the Asuza Street gatherings stating: 'Three days of fasting and prayer were set apart at the Mission for more power in the meetings. The Lord answered and souls were slain all about the altar the second night. We have felt an increase of power every night'[32] which resulted in many new converts and churches planted.

Fasting, then, is missional. It is not only good for our bodies (chapter one); it not only helps us become more holy (chapter two); it not only needs practising wisely and well (chapter three); and it not only empowers intercession (chapter four). It also sends us out as God's missionary disciples.

Discipleship

Discipleship is the daily practice of following Jesus. It is not only the best way to live but it's also the means by which we bring transformation to the world, for all disciples are meant to be people of mission. The message of Christ – the good news of the 'gospel' which we carry is not meant to be kept to ourselves but shared with others, through our words and actions. To do this, we need all sorts of help. That's why we're always called to discipleship in community for we all need the support of the church, the family of God, as a home for friendship, worship and mission. We also require the help of the Holy Spirit to empower us 'in our weakness'.[33] He does this in all sorts of ways, especially as we live generously, prayerfully and fast – which are the three core discipleship habits Jesus taught in the Sermon on the Mount.

Missionary disciples are meant to be disciplined, practising good habits. In my short book *The A-Z of Discipleship* in 'D is for Discipline', I say: 'To excel in any field requires discipline. It's the same when it comes to discipleship. The ones that mature well and are most effective are the disciplined ones. In fact, one simple definition of "disciple" is *disciplined one.*'[34] This book has shown that a key discipline for missionary disciples is fasting, which explains why some traditions of the church have insisted on it. After all, if you want to be an effective disciple, it makes sense to start fasting. However, a careful reading of Scripture shows that while fasting is highly commended, it is not universally commanded. That means we don't *have* to fast, in the same way that we also don't *have* to give, or even pray. Instead, we're *invited* to. It really is an invitation. But it's not an ordinary invitation. It's an invitation from the King of kings that the wise will not turn down. It's not unlike being invited by the monarch to Buckingham Palace with an invitation marked 'RSVP'. While you *could* turn it down, the expectation is that you will say, 'Yes, of course, I'd be honoured.' Fasting is like that, but more important. We're not told we must, but it's assumed we will. The choice is ours.

Jesus assumes we will fast, not because he is cruel but because he is kind. He has great plans for us and his world, and he wants to use us to see them fulfilled in our day. He has many sick bodies he wants to heal; many broken people he wants to draw into his kingdom; many divided families he wants to unite, and many war-torn places where he wants to bring peace. We can't make that happen, but empowered by his Holy Spirit, as his prayerful fasting people, we can.

Perhaps Lou Engle is right when he makes the bold statement that 'Fasting is the greatest power for the shifting of history.'[35] If he is, that might explain why St Augustine, many years before him, said 'Fasting, therefore, is very necessary'[36] and why we need to learn *The Art of Fasting*, not only for own wellbeing, but for the sake of the world.

Simon

Simon is a missionary disciple of Jesus and a church leader involved in church planting. He started to fast by observing others, beginning small. He recently wrote to me his story:

I have been a church leader for over twenty years and fasting has been my key spiritual discipline. I was first exposed to it during a visit to the Redeemed Christian Church of God in Lagos, Nigeria, where I was introduced to church leaders and regular church members who were routinely going about their day-to-day business and yet had been fasting for several weeks. This experience made a lasting impression on me and I privately began journeying with God in this area. Over time I moved past a single day fast to three days, one week, ten days, three weeks and beyond. I have now completed five forty-day fasts where as much as is possible I seek to hold on to the regular responsibilities and rhythms of everyday life – both as a parent and church leader.

The key spiritual benefit I have received from the practice of fasting is the provision of valuable time that it frees up so that I can spend more time with the Lord. In particular, these times always provide an immensely valuable means of crucially needed spiritual reset. I do not regularly keep a journal but always do so during fasting periods as these times generally prove so rich, liberating and reorientating. During my years as [a church leader], and now in a church planting capacity [in my church], the focus of my ministry has always been inclined towards the most marginalised (e.g. homeless, those in addiction and recovery, ex-offenders, asylum seekers, etc.) and fasting has been so crucial in sustaining my commitment to this – despite all the challenges involved. It would not be overstating it to say that without my practising of this discipline I do not think I would have been able to have sustained this outward focus, particularly alongside the wider pressures of ministry and family life.

While the focus, clarity and resetting nature of fasting have been the standout benefits of the discipline for me, I have also experienced some occasions of spiritual breakthrough in wider circumstances. A standout example of this was in 2017 when I was team leader of [N Church] and subsequent to completing a forty-day fast which was both for personal refreshing and greater spiritual breakthrough in our local community, we very soon afterwards went into an unexpected season as a church where we became a real place of belonging for those with addiction issues and those recently out of prison. Several of these individuals came to faith and were baptised and continue to walk with the Lord today. We subsequently set up two houses in partnership with [a charity] for these individuals. There is no doubt in my mind that some measure of breakthrough was achieved through my private fasting, with a more public and important consequence of the fast also being that halfway through, I felt it right to establish a daily midday prayer meeting at the church which also focused on praying for the community and proved invaluable in carrying us into further breakthrough.

Another missional consequence of fasting beyond a generally heightened sense of the Lord's presence when engaging in different forms of ministry, has also been when I have been doing longer fasts and have chosen to share this with Muslims. I have regularly sensed the working of the Lord at such times . . . and I have been able to point [them] to the strength and power of Jesus. On several occasions I have also intentionally combined my periods of fasting alongside Ramadan.

My 'go to' scripture when I fast is: *'Sow for yourselves righteousness, reap the fruit of unfailing love; and break up your unploughed ground, for it is time to seek the LORD, until he comes and showers righteousness on you'* (Hosea 10:12). This emphasis serves to anchor me in my periods of fasting and provides a platform for the spiritual reset and restoration which I find so crucial in sustaining me to live an outward-facing life.[37]

As I observe the church in the West, like many I recognise that our missional impact needs to increase. Mission really should be at the heart of our lives and churches, being the reason we exist. Bishop Lesslie Newbigin knew this, famously saying that 'a church that is not "the church in mission" is no church at all'.[38] That's why fasting has to prayerfully and intentionally go from our mouth, through our heart and hands, touching our knees and empowering our feet, for that's how real change comes. We really do, as Rebecca Solnit says, 'write history with our feet'.[39]

So put on your gospel shoes and step out in mission as Christ's ambassador, empowered by prayerful fasting, recognising that Mark Batterson is probably right when he says, 'An empty stomach may be the most powerful prayer posture in Scripture.'[40]

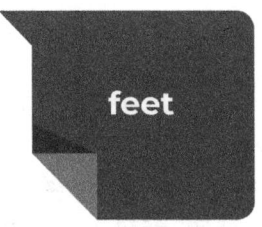

- fasting turns holy feet into missionary feet
- fasting should always have a missionary impact
- fasting is modelled by leaders
- fasting is commended to all disciples
- fasting empowers God's church for mission

Afterword

- *'When you fast . . .' (Matthew 6:16; Jesus Christ).*[1]

- *'The Scriptures bid us to fast; the Church says* Now*' (George Herbert).*[2]

Fasting is the spiritual discipline that is *most misunderstood*.[3] Saints of old believed this was because Satan trembles at the very thought of us fasting, and so he does all he can to confuse us. I hope this book has brought some clarity as to what fasting is and why it's important.

Fasting is the spiritual discipline that is *most mis-applied*. It's so easy to start with good intentions but end up become legalistic or even feeling proud of our fasting endeavours, which goes against one of its core aims, which is to humble us.

Fasting is the spiritual discipline that is *most mis-managed*. Many take the discipline far too lightly, while some are too strict.

Fasting is the spiritual discipline that is *most mis-directed*. Many practise it just for themselves without realising its effects are meant to go way beyond us and benefit others.

And yet fasting is the spiritual discipline that is meant to be *most mis-sional*! As we've seen in our final chapter, fasting energises action, empowers prayers and equips disciples for missionary service in the world God loves so much.

So, with fresh understanding, let's practise. Again and again. For if we can learn once more to be a people who practise *The Art of Fasting*, then the future is gloriously hopeful.

Acknowledgements

This book is dedicated to my brother and sister-in-law, William and Karen Porter. William and Karen, you have modelled prayer and fasting and a humble prayerful disposition to me, like no others. You have selflessly served God and his church, praying and fasting through good and difficult times, and especially as you have led the Beacon House of Prayer in Stoke-in-Trent for more than twenty years. I honour you in this book.

I am so grateful to those who read initial manuscripts of this book, sharing their wisdom and reflections and making it better. These include James Fletcher, Rachael Franklin, Sheila Jacobs and Sam Porter. Thank you.

Resources

On Habits

James Clear, *Atomic Habits* (New York: Penguin, 2018).

Wendy Wood, *Good Habits, Bad Habits* (New York: Farrar, Straus and Giroux, 2019).

On Spiritual Disciplines

John Mark Comer, *Practicing the Way* (London: SPCK, 2024).

Richard Foster, *Celebration of Discipline* (London: Hodder & Stoughton, 1989).

Mary Margaret Funk, *Tools Matter for Practicing the Spiritual Life* (New York, NY: Continuum, 2001).

Andrew Roberts, *Holy Habits* (Malcolm Down Publishing, 2016).

Dallas Willard, *The Spirit of the Disciplines* (New York: HarperOne, 1991).

On Fasting

Orthodox:

Saint Basil the Great, *On Fasting and Feasting* (Yonkers, NY: St Vladimir's Seminary Press, 2013).

Catholic:

Dag Tessore, *Fasting* (London: New City, 2007).

Anglican:

Scot McKnight, *Fasting* (Nashville, TN: Thomas Nelson, 2009).

Methodist:

https://worldmethodist.org/prayer-and-fasting/ accessed 23rd April 2024.

Pentecostal:

Jennifer A. Miskov, *Fasting for Fire* (Shippensburg, PA: Destiny Image, 2021).

General:

David Bolster and Anna de Lange, *Fasting: A Fresh Look at an Old Discipline – Spirituality Series 83* (Cambridge: Grove Books, 2002).

Lee Roy Martin, *Fasting: A Centre for Pentecostal Theology Short Introduction* (Cleveland, TN: CPT Press, 2014).

John Piper, *A Hunger for God* (Leicester: IVP, 1997).

Matthew Porter, *Spiritual Discipline & Leadership Formation – Renewal Series 21* (Cambridge: Grove Books, 2005).

Matthew Porter, *The A–Z of Prayer* (Milton Keynes: Authentic Media, 2019).

Arthur Wallis, *God's Chosen Fast* (Eastbourne: Kingsway, 1968).

Notes

Preface

[1] Matthew 11:28–30, *The Message*.

Introduction

[1] These include: Lynn Hardy, *The Fasting Bible: How to Lose Weight, Grow Younger and Heal Your Body (In 30 Days or Less)* (Independently published, 2022); Olivia Rivers, *Intermittent Fasting Book: The Proven Method For Achieving Longevity, Efficient Weight Loss, and Optimal Health* (London: Alsworthy Press, 2023) and Gin Stephens, *Fast. Feast. Repeat.* (London: Macmillan, 2020).

[2] https://medium.com/illumination/how-many-years-do-you-spend-eating-3f6971a80e46 (accessed 12th March 2024).

[3] The average person spends half the time cooking as their parents' generation. See https://www.independent.co.uk/life-style/home-cooking-meal-time-kitchen-microwave-parents-a9361236.html (accessed 12th March 2024).

[4] I've believed this for a while, first writing about fasting twenty years ago and its strategic place in our lives, especially for leaders. See Matthew Porter, *Spiritual Discipline & Leadership Formation – Renewal Series 21* (Cambridge: Grove Books, 2005).

[5] Jennifer A. Miskov, *Fasting for Fire* (Shippensburg, PA: Destiny Image, 2021), p.112.

[6] Dietrich Bonhoeffer, *The Cost of Discipleship* (London: SCM Press, 1959), p.151. Bonhoeffer (1906–45) was a German theologian and martyr.

[7] Many writers on fasting have fasted while writing on the subject, including Scot McKnight, *Fasting* (Nashville, TN: Thomas Nelson, 2009), p.16.

[8] This is the title of Dallas Willard's important 1988 book. See Dallas Willard, *The Spirit of the Disciplines* (New York: HarperOne, 1991).

[9] Scot McKnight, *Fasting*, p.2.

[10] Writing in 2009 McKnight said that 'your body image opens a window into your spirituality' and rightly said that: 'Until we have a healthier body image . . . it is not likely that body talk (fasting) will occur as it should' (McKnight, *Fasting*, pp.11–12).

Chapter 1

[1] John Chrysostom, cited in Cotton Mather, *The Great Works of Christ in America*, vol. 2 (Edinburgh: The Banner of Truth Trust, 1979; orig. 1702), p.148.

[2] Mark Batterson, *The Circle Maker* (Grand Rapids: Zondervan, 2011), p.165. Mark Batterson is an American pastor and prolific author.

[3] Rolland and Heidi Baker, *Always Enough* (Grand Rapids, MI: Baker, 2003), p.165.

[4] Heidi Baker, *Compelled by Love* (Lake Mary, FL: Charisma House, 2008), p.101.

[5] Baker, *Compelled by Love*, p.59.

[6] See Luke 21:1–4

[7] Matthew Porter, *The Art of Giving* (Milton Keynes: Authentic Media, 2024), p.12.

[8] See, for example, 2 Kings 4:1–11; Luke 18:1–8.

[9] *The Problem of Pain* by CS Lewis © copyright 1940 CS Lewis Pte Ltd. Extract used with permission.

[10] John Piper, *A Hunger for God* (Leicester: IVP, 1997), p.9.

[11] https://www.nhs.uk/common-health-questions/food-and-diet/what-should-my-daily-intake-of-calories-be/ (accessed 16th February 2024). Calorie intake can also depend on other factors including someone's age, lifestyle and size, and this can also be impacted by our hormones and whether we are on medication or unwell.

[12] Some see the pictures of food and eating in Revelation as metaphorical, given that Revelation 7:16 speaks of eternity being a place of no hunger or thirst, but even if that is the case, Revelation speaks positively about food and feasting.

[13] Proverbs 3:9.

[14] Luke 7:34.

[15] Luke 22:16; Matthew 26:7ff; Mark 14:8ff; Luke 22:14ff.

[16] There are all sorts of fascinating studies on this, including the helpful book: Ken Albala and Trudy Eden, eds, *Food and Faith* (New York: Columbia University Press, 2011).

[17] Basil the Great, *Longer Rules* 19 (trans. Anna M. Silvas; Collegeville, MN: Liturgical Press, 2013).

[18] See https://alpha.org.uk/ (accessed 22nd July 2024).

[19] https://www.bbcgoodfood.com/howto/guide/health-benefits-fasting (accessed 17th February 2024). Edited and paraphrased for the purposes of this book.

[20] Miskov, *Fasting for Fire*, p.96.

[21] Thomas Aquinas, Summa Theologica (II, 2, Q 147, Art 1).

[22] Cyril of Jerusalem, *Homily on the Paralytic,* XVIII. To be fair to the Catholic tradition, when it comes to fasting, there is much more to it than just negativity towards our sinful human nature, as Dag Tessore's helpful book *Fasting* shows, which I commend to all who want to dig deeper. See Dag Tessore, *Fasting* (London: New City, 2007).

[23] 2 Corinthians 12:9–10.

[24] Willard, *The Spirit of the Disciplines*, p.138.

[25] Willard, *The Spirit of the Disciplines*, p.167.

[26] The New Testament calls this *kenosis,* which is best translated as 'self-emptying'. It is beautifully described in Philippians 2:6–11. For more on *kenosis,* see 'K is for Kenosis' in Matthew Porter, *A–Z of Prayer* (Milton Keynes: Authentic Media, 2019), pp.79–85.

[27] John 6:38.

[28] Matthew 3:16.

[29] Adalbert de Vogüé, *To Love Fasting: The Monastic Experience* (Petersham, MA: St Bede's Publications, 1989), p.8.

[30] Matthew 6:11.

[31] These (i.e. social action and social justice) are Marks 3 and 4 of 'Five Marks of Mission' of the Anglican Communion. See https://www.anglicancommunion.org/mission/marks-of-mission.aspx (accessed 18th February 2024).

[32] See Rodney Stark, *The Triumph of Christianity* (New York: HarperCollins, 2011), pp.112ff.

[33] See Alan Kreider, *The Patient Ferment of the Early Church* (Grand Rapids, MI: Baker Academic, 2016), pp.1155ff.

[34] Clement of Alexandria, 'The Instructor' 3.12, in *Ante-Nicene Fathers*, vol. 2 (eds Alexander Roberts and James Donaldson; Peabody, MA: Hendrickson, 1885, 1994), pp.292–293.

[35] Aristedes, *Apology*, 15, https://www.newadvent.org/fathers/1012.htm (accessed 30 July 2024).

[36] Hermas, *Similitudes*, v.3.7, in *Ante-Nicene Fathers*, vol. 2 (eds Roberts and Donaldson), p.34.

[37] Origen, 'Homily 10 on Leviticus', in *The Fathers of the Church,* vol. 83 (trans. Gary Wayne Barkley; Washington DC: The Catholic University of America Press, 1990), p.207.

[38] John 6:35.

[39] Willard, *The Spirit of the Disciplines*, p.166.

[40] Lou Engle, 'The Bridegroom Fast' in Miskov, *Fasting for Fire*, p.61.
[41] 1 Corinthians 13:12, kjv.
[42] Psalm 34:8.

Chapter 2

[1] Miskov, *Fasting for Fire*, p.71. Miskov is a revival historian, speaker and itinerant minister based in the United States.
[2] https://daviddocusen.com/a-review-of-isaiah-581-14-gods-heart-for-equity-and-justice/ (accessed 11 November 2024). Docusen is a US pastor, executive coach and blogger.
[3] See John Wesley, *The Journal of the Rev. John Wesley* (London: The Epworth Press, 1938), p.147.
[4] Joel 2:12.
[5] Brené Brown, *Dare to Lead* (New York: Random House, 2018), p.72.
[6] For example, in Psalm 20:4.
[7] The aim is for our hearts to become aligned with God's hearts. See, for example, Psalm 37:4.
[8] James K.A. Smith, *You Are What You Love* (Grand Rapids, MI: Brazos Press, 2016), p.16.
[9] Smith, *You Are What You Love*, p.19.
[10] Johannes Hartl, *Heart Fire* (Edinburgh: Muddy Pearl, 2018), p.57.
[11] John 6:69.
[12] John Stott, cited in R. Steere, *Church on Fire* (London: Hodder & Stoughton, 1998), p.454.
[13] Saint Basil the Great, 'First Homily on Fasting' in *On Fasting and Feasting* (Yonkers, New York: St Vladimir's Seminary Press, 2013), p.62.
[14] Piper, *A Hunger for God*, p.135.
[15] Saint Basil the Great, 'Second Homily on Fasting' in *On Fasting and Feasting*, pp.75–76.

16. 2 Corinthians 3:18.
17. John Chrysostom, *The Homilies of the Statutes to the People of Antioch* (trans. W.R.W. Stephens; Homily III.9, in Philip Schaff, ed, *Nicene and Post-Nicene Fathers, First Series*, vol. 9; Peabody, MA: Hendrickson, 1889, 1995), p.359.
18. Richard Foster, *Celebration of Discipline* (London: Hodder & Stoughton, 1980, 1989), p.69.
19. Miskov, *Fasting for Fire*, p.9.
20. Citing Psalm 104:4.
21. Saint Basil the Great, 'First Homily on Fasting' in *On Fasting and Feasting*, p.55.
22. Origen, 'Homily 10 on Leviticus', in *The Fathers of the Church*, vol. 83, p.206.
23. From the Lord's Prayer from Church of England's Common Worship, © The Archbishops' Council of the Church of England. https://www.churchofengland.org/prayer-and-worship/worship-texts-and-resources/common-worship/common-material/lords-prayer (accessed 26th July 2024).
24. N.T. Wright, *Simply Christian* (New York: HarperOne, 2010), p.148.
25. St Athanasius, in letter to Marcellinus, cited in Tim Keller, *Prayer* (London: Hodder & Stoughton, 2014), p.255.
26. Paula Gooder, *Journalling the Psalms* (London: Hodder & Stoughton, 2022), p.1.
27. James 4:8, NRSVA.
28. Mary Margaret Funk, *Tools Matter for Practicing the Spiritual Life* (New York, NY: Continuum, 2001), p.56.
29. Romans 12:2.
30. Philippians 4:8.
31. 2 Corinthians 2:16.
32. Ephesians 1:17.
33. Keller, *Prayer*, p.165.

[34] Martin Luther King, *A Gift of Love* (London: Penguin, 1963, 2012, 2017), p.6.

[35] Miskov, *Fasting for Fire*, p.71.

[36] James K.A. Smith, *You Are What You Love*, p.85.

[37] Miskov, *Fasting for Fire*, pp.81–82.

[38] Matthew Porter, *The Art of Journalling* (Milton Keynes: Authentic Media, 2024).

[39] 1 Samuel 13:13; see Acts 13:22.

[40] Samuel Chadwick, *The Path of Prayer* (London: Hodder & Stoughton, 1931), p.18.

[41] Leonard Ravenhill, *Why Revival Tarries* (Bloomington, MN: Bethany House, 1959, 1987), p.25.

[42] Proverbs 4:23, NIV 1984.

[43] Matthew 6:13.

[44] Saint Basil the Great, 'Second Homily on Fasting' in *On Fasting and Feasting*, p.74.

[45] Andrew Fuller (1754–1815, English Baptist pastor), *The Complete Works of the Rev. Andrew Fuller*, vol. 1 (Harrisonburg, VA: Sprinkle Publications, 1988, orig. 1844), p.583.

Chapter 3

[1] Brown, *Dare to Lead*, pp.5–6.

[2] Willian Dryness, cited in Fujimura, *Art & Faith*, p.85. Dryness is a theologian of theology and culture at Fuller Theological Seminary, Pasadena in the USA.

[3] https://rushtopress.org/bono-quotes-petersons-message-bible/ (accessed 27th July 2024).

[4] Ezekiel 3:3. Jeremiah does something similar, saying in 15:16 that 'When your words came, I ate them.'

[5] Revelation 10:9–10.

Notes

[6] Eugene Peterson, *Eat This Book* (London: Hodder & Stoughton, 2006), xi.

[7] We designated Thursdays 'Prayer Day' at St Chad's, and invited people to join us at one prayer event if they could: 9 a.m. Morning Prayer, 11 a.m. Holy Communion, 2 p.m. Prayer Meeting, 7 p.m. Prayer Meeting.

[8] Nicholas Sagovsky, 'Foreword' to Dag Tessore, *Fasting*, p.14.

[9] https://www.shatinchurch.org.hk/fasting/ (accessed 23rd April 2024).

[10] Saint Basil the Great, 'First Homily on Fasting' in *On Fasting and Feasting*, p.67.

[11] See 1 Corinthians 7:5.

[12] 1 Corinthians 8:13.

[13] Numbers 6:1–21.

[14] Luke 1:15.

[15] Apart from communion wine I do not drink alcohol. I don't seek to be legalistic about this, and will eat food that contains alcohol. I'm also not uncomfortable having people around me drinking alcohol; it's just I don't drink it myself.

[16] The Scriptures teach, and church history affirms that Christian marriage is for heterosexual couples. Not all Christians believe this today, with various denominations recently extending marriage to same-sex couples, as has happened in the civil marriages of many Western nations.

[17] See Matthew 4:1–11.

[18] Porter, *The Art of Journalling*, p.38.

[19] Dietrich Bonhoeffer said that 'All the prayers of Holy Scripture are summarised in the Lord's Prayer' (Bonhoeffer, *Psalms: The Prayer Book of the Bible*, p.16).

[20] https://www.churchofengland.org/prayer-and-worship/worship-texts-and-resources/common-worship/common-material/lords-prayer (accessed 29th July 2024).

21 David Watson, *One in the Spirit* (London: Hodder & Stoughton, 1973), p.53.
22 'Speaking in tongues' is a Spirit-given ability to speak in an unlearned language of prayer to God. For more on this, see 'T is for Tongues' in Porter, *The A–Z of Prayer*, pp.149–156.
23 Jill Duff, *Lighting the Beacons* (London: SPCK, 2023), p.98.
24 Matthew 4:4.
25 Heidi Baker, 'I'm not a Drug Dealer. I promise!' in Miskov, *Fasting for Fire*, p.96.
26 Saint Basil the Great, 'First Homily on Fasting' in *On Fasting and Feasting*, p.64.
27 For more on this, see 'N is for Nights' in Porter, *The A–Z of Prayer*, pp.101–107.
28 Saint Basil the Great, 'First Homily on Fasting' in *On Fasting and Feasting*, p.63.
29 Fourth-century St Ambrose taught this, saying, 'When thou fastest, boast not thyself, nor brag not of it.' Cited in Thomas Becon, https://www.anglican.net/works/thomas-becon-a-fruitful-treatise-of-fasting-wherein-is-declared-what-the-christian-fast-is-how-we-ought-to-fast-what-the-true-use-of-fasting-is-1551/ (accessed 8th July 2024), p.18 of 28.
30 Jonathan Edwards, 'Some Thoughts Concerning the Revival', in *The Works of Jonathan Edwards,* vol. 4 (New Haven, CT: Yale University Press, 1972), p.507.
31 Randy Clark, 'God's Chosen Fast', in Miskov, *Fasting for Fire*, p.65.
32 Becon, *A Fruitful Treatise*, p.27 of 28.

Chapter 4

1 Source unknown but widely attributed to Corrie ten Boom. Corrie ten Boom (1892–1983) was a Dutch Christian and speaker, who helped many Dutch Jews escape from Nazi persecution, was

arrested and incarcerated in Ravenbrück concentration camp. Her story was written up in the best-selling book *The Hiding Place* (Uhrichsville, OH: Barbour Books, 1971).

2. Batterson, *The Circle Maker*, p.150.

3. For more on this, see https://mwerickson.com/2019/08/29/old-camel-knees-a-brief-reflection-on-the-remarkable-prayer-life-of-james-the-just/ (accessed 2nd April 2024).

4. Widely attributed to Thomas Guthrie (1803–73), who was a Scottish divine of the Victorian era. See https://www.gracegems.org/30/gems_from_guthrie.htm (accessed 4th April 2024).

5. John Wesley, *The Works of the Rev. John Wesley*, XIII (London: Wesleyan-Methodist Bookroom, 1872), p.7.

6. Wesley, *The Works of the Rev. John Wesley*, XIII, p.396.

7. Lee Roy Martin, *Fasting: A Centre for Pentecostal Theology Short Introduction* (Cleveland, TN: CPT Press, 2014), p.112.

8. See Matthew 3:13ff.

9. Wesley, *The Journal of the Rev. John Wesley*, VII, p. 360. Also, when asked in a 1787 letter about persecution of Methodists in the Channel Islands, Wesley replied that 'the best method to be used in this exigence is fasting and prayer' (John Wesley, *The Works of the Rev. John Wesley*, XIII, p.8).

10. Dietrich Bonhoeffer wrote: 'As soon as a Christian recognizes that he has failed in his service, that his readiness has become feeble, and that he has sinned against another's life and become guilty of another's guilt, that all his joy in God has vanished and that his capacity for prayer has quite gone, it is high time for him to launch an assault upon the flesh, and prepare for better service by fasting and prayer.' Bonhoeffer, *The Cost of Discipleship*, p.152.

11. Engle, 'The Bridegroom Fast,' Chapter 6 in Miskov, *Fasting for Fire*, p.184.

12. Miskov, *Fasting for Fire*, p.106.

[13] Miskov, *Fasting for Fire*, p.12. Her italics.
[14] Widely attributed to Moody, although source unknown.
[15] https://www.dci.org.uk/zipped/ReesHowells-Intercessor.pdf (accessed 13th April 2024).
[16] Miskov, *Fasting for Fire*, p.66.
[17] *Didache*, 1:3 https://www.newadvent.org/fathers/0714.htm (accessed 27th July 2024).
[18] Saint Basil the Great, 'Second Homily on Fasting' in *On Fasting and Feasting*, p.77.
[19] Laceye Warner, 'Spreading Scriptural Holiness: Theology and Practices of Early Methodism for the Contemporary Church', *The Asbury Journal*, 63/1:115–138, https://place.asburyseminary.edu/cgi/viewcontent.cgi?article=1076&context=asburyjournal (accessed 31st May 2024), © 2008 Asbury Theological Seminar.
[20] Scot McKnight, *Fasting*, p.123.
[21] John Piper, *A Hunger for God*, p.83.
[22] 2 Peter 3:12.
[23] Missiologist Steve Addison notes this in *The Rise and Fall of Movements* (Cody, WY: 100 Movements Publishing, 2019), as does Alan Hirsch recognising that in 1860 American Methodism 'no longer required classes and bands' and the centrality of prayer began to wane, for 'discipleship had become an optional extra. Methodism has been in decline ever since!' (Alan Hirsch, 'Afterword' in Winfield Bevins, *Marks of a Movement* (Grand Rapids, MI: Zondervan, 2019), p.185.
[24] See https://ontheruinofbritain.wordpress.com/2019/03/20/john-wesley-on-reading-the-early-church-fathers/ (accessed 8th April 2024).
[25] John Chrysostom, cited in Cotton Mather, *The Great Works of Christ in America*, vol. 2 (Edinburgh: The Banner of Truth Trust, 1979, orig. 1702), p.148.
[26] Matthew 4:11.
[27] Daniel 10:12.

[28] 1 Kings 19:1–8.

[29] Saint Basil the Great, 'First Homily on Fasting' in *On Fasting and Feasting*, p.63.

[30] Saint Basil the Great, 'Second Homily on Fasting' in *On Fasting and Feasting*, p.74.

[31] https://www.patheos.com/blogs/catholicbookblogger/2017/04/19/fasting-makes-us-angels-prayer-comes-angels-day-270/ (accessed 4th April 2024).

[32] Saint Basil the Great, 'Second Homily on Fasting' in *On Fasting and Feasting*, p.78.

[33] For Muslims, see https://lifewithallah.com/articles/seasons-of-worship/ramadan/in-the-company-of-the-angels/ (accessed 4th April 2024). For Jews, see https://www.thejc.com/judaism/become-an-angel-for-a-day-by-fasting-on-yom-kippur-pak97v5e (accessed 4th April 2024).

[34] Basil expressed it in this way: 'if the angels have any food, it is bread, as the Prophet says, *Man ate the bread of angels*' – which is a reference to Psalm 78:25. Saint Basil the Great, 'First Homily on Fasting' in *On Fasting and Feasting*, p.68.

[35] Saint Basil the Great, 'Second Homily on Fasting' in *On Fasting and Feasting*, p.74.

[36] Bill Johnson, of Bethel Church in Redding, California may well be right when he makes the interesting observation: 'I believe angels have been bored because we live the kind of lifestyle that doesn't require much of their help. Their assignment is to assist us in supernatural endeavours' (Bill Johnson, *When Heaven Invades Earth* [Shippensburg, PA: Destiny Image, 2003], p.139).

[37] The phrase 'the king of angels' is well known to all who sing carols at Christmas, appearing in the hymn *O Come All Ye Faithful*, which is variously attributed to John Francis Wade (1711–86), John Reading (1645–92), King John IV of Portugal (1604–56), as well as anonymous Cistercian monks.

[38] Pete Greig, *Dirty Glory* (London: Hodder & Stoughton, 2016), p.120.

Chapter 5

1. Attributed to St Augustine. Cited in Michael Yankoski, *The Sacred Year* (Nashville, TN: Thomas Nelson, 2014), p.209.
2. Rebecca Solnit, *Hope in the Dark* (London: Canongate, 2016), xxiii. Solnit is an American secular author, writing particularly in the fields of feminism, Western and indigenous history and popular power.
3. https://cbfblog.com/2018/01/15/martin-luther-king-jr-day-2018-a-time-for-self-purification/ (accessed 5th April 2024).
4. https://emeth.net/praying-with-my-feet/ (accessed 27th July 2024).
5. John Chrysostom, *The Homilies of the Statutes to the People of Antioch* (trans. W.R.W. Stephens; Homily III.9, in Philip Schaff, ed, *Nicene and Post-Nicene Fathers, First Series*, vol. 9), p.359. As part of this sermon, Chrysostom lists various body parts and applies them to fasting, grasping that fasting really is body-prayer.
6. See Exodus 3ff.
7. Isaiah 6:1–8.
8. See Peter's calling in Luke 5:1–11, which includes Peter saying: 'Go away from me, Lord; I am a sinful man!'
9. John 13:14.
10. John Jewel, in *Certain Sermons or Homilies Appointed to be Read in Churches in the Time of Queen Elizabeth of Famous Memory*, originally published in 1562 (London: SPCK, 1864).
11. https://www.pewresearch.org/religion/2011/12/19/global-christianity-movements-and-denominations/ (accessed 14th April 2024). This number includes about 280 million Pentecostals and more than 300 million 'charismatics' who are part of other Christians denominations but would share a similar spirituality.
12. *Apostolic Faith* 1.4 (Dec. 1906), p.1.
13. A.J. Tomlinson, *The Last Great Conflict* (The Church of God Movement Heritage Series; Cleveland, TN: White Wing Publishing House, 2011), p.139.

14. Martin, *Fasting*, p.117.
15. Martin, *Fasting*, p.144.
16. Martin, *Fasting*, p.144.
17. Matthew Porter, *The A–Z of Discipleship* (Milton Keynes: Authentic Media, 2017), p.24.
18. See https://www.proquest.com/openview/6d81c91507ecc60e21a5678fab19309e/1.pdf?pq-origsite=gscholar&cbl=18750&diss=y (accessed 8th April 2024), and https://place.asburyseminary.edu/ecommonsatsdissertations/1542/ (accessed 8th April 2024).
19. Steve Addison, *Movements that Change the World: Five Keys to Spreading the Gospel.* (Smyrna, DE: Missional Press, 2009), p.46; Steve Addison, *Pioneering Movements: Leadership That Multiplies Disciples and Churches* (Leicester: IVP, 2015), pp.54, 84; Steve Addison, *The Rise and Fall of Movements*, p.61; Winfield Bevins, *Marks of a Movement*, pp.47, 183.
20. There is much anecdotal evidence for this, and a growing body of empirical evidence. See, for example: https://www.sciencedirect.com/science/article/pii/S2444569X22000440 (accessed 11th April 2024).
21. Becon, *A Fruitful Treatise of Fasting*, p.3 of 28.
22. Saint Basil the Great, 'First Homily on Fasting' in *On Fasting and Feasting*, p.61.
23. Augustine, *Epistolae*, LIV, 6, pp.7–8.
24. See Luke 6:12–13.
25. Acts 14:23.
26. Acts 1:8.
27. Acts 1:14.
28. See Acts 2:1ff.
29. *Church of God Evangel* 6.39 (25 Sept 1915), p.3.
30. Martin, *Fasting*, p.94.
31. Martin, *Fasting*, p.170.

[32] Asuza Street Mission (May 1907), in 'At Asuza Mission', *The Apostolic Faith* 1:8 (May 1907).

[33] Romans 8:26.

[34] Porter, *The A–Z of Discipleship*, p.23.

[35] Miskov, *Fasting for Fire*, p.120.

[36] Cited in Becon, *A Fruitful Treatise of Fasting*, p.21 of 28.

[37] Edited for the purposes of this book.

[38] Lesslie Newbigin, *The Open Secret* (Grand Rapids, MI: Eerdmans, 1978, 1995), p.2.

[39] Solnit, *Hope in the Dark* (London: Canongate, 2016), p.xxiii.

[40] Batterson, *The Circle Maker*, p.165.

Afterword

[1] Matthew 6:16.

[2] George Herbert, *The Works of George Herbert in Prose and Verse*, vol. II (London: Bell and Daldy, 1859), p.91.

[3] I agree with theologian and pastor Scot McKnight, who says: 'fasting is the most misunderstood of the Christian spiritual disciplines' (McKnight, *Fasting*, xii).

Index of People

Aquinas, Thomas 26, 133
Aristedes, of Athens 32
Athanasius, of Alexandria 55
Augustine, of Hippo 122, 134, 142
Baker, Heidi 12, 25, 86
Basil, the Great 19, 48, 54, 65, 79, 117, 150
Batterson, Mark 12, 102, 146
Becon, Thomas 96, 134
Bonhoeffer, Dietrich 4, 159, 161
Brown, Brené 45, 70
Brown, Pearl Page 131
Chadwick, Samuel 64
Chrysostom, John 12, 51, 116, 124
Clark, Randy 94
Clement, of Alexandria 32
Cyril, of Jerusalem 26
Docusen, David 42
Dryness, William 70
Duff, Jill 86
Engle, Lou 34, 108, 142
Foster, Richard 51, 150
Fuller, Andrew 66
Funk, Margaret 57
Gooder, Paula 55
Guthrie, Thomas 104, 161
Hameed, Saira 1
Hartl, Johannes 46
Hegesippus, Nazarine 102
Herbert, George 147
Hermas, Shepherd of 32
Heschel, Abraham J. 123
Howells, Rees 111
James, the Just 103
Jewel, John 128
John XIII, Pope 27
Keller, Tim 58
King, Martin Luther 59, 122
Kreider, Alan 31
Lewis, Charles Staples 16
Lowe, Paul 110
Martin, Lee Roy 105, 130, 131, 140, 151
McKnight, Scot 7, 114, 151, 166
Miskov, Jennifer 42, 52, 59, 60, 109, 112
Moody, D.L. 110
Nazirites 80
Newbigin, Lesslie 145
Origen, of Alexandria 33, 54
Perry, Samuel C. 137
Peterson, Eugene v, 70
Piper, John 16, 48, 114, 151
Ravenhill, Leonard 64
Sagovsky, Nicholas 76
Sentamu, John 75
Seymour, William 130
Solnit, Rebecca 122, 146
Stott, John 48
Ten Boom, Corrie 102
Vogüé, de, Adalbert 29
Watson, David 85
Wesley, John 43, 104, 106, 113, 116
Willard, Dallas 6, 27, 34, 150
Wright, Tom 55

The Art of Giving

Becoming a more generous person

Matthew Porter

978-1-78893-290-5

The Art of Journalling

Becoming a more reflective person

Matthew Porter

978-1-78893-288-2

The Art of … is a series of books about discipleship habits.

In each book a spiritual habit is explained and explored in an accessible way, and you are encouraged to practise this art through practical pointers and exercises. By developing these holy habits, you can become a more fruitful and fulfilled missional disciple of Jesus.

www.ingramcontent.com/pod-product-compliance
Lightning Source LLC
LaVergne TN
LVHW051121080426
835510LV00018B/2158